W9-DDY-571

Rediscovering the Lord's Prayer

by Art Simon

Augsburg Books
MINNEAPOLIS

REDISCOVERING THE LORD'S PRAYER

Copyright © 2005 Arthur Simon. All rights reserved. Except for brief quotations in critical articles or reviews, no part of this book may be reproduced in any manner without prior written permission from the publisher. Write to: Permissions, Augsburg Fortress, Box 1209, Minneapolis, MN 55440.

Large-quantity purchases or custom editions of this book are available at a discount from the publisher. For more information, contact the sales department at Augsburg Fortress, Publishers, 1-800-328-4648, or write to: Sales Director, Augsburg Fortress, Publishers, P. O. Box 1209, Minneapolis, MN 55440-1209.

Scripture passages, unless otherwise marked, are from the New Revised Standard Version of the Bible, copyright © 1946, 1952, 1971, 1989 by the Division of Christian Education of the National Council of the Churches of Christ in the USA. Used by permission.

    Scripture passages marked NIV are from the Holy Bible, New International Version, copyright © 1973, 1978, 1984 International Bible Society. Used by permission of Zondervan Publishing House. All rights reserved.

    Scripture passages marked RSV are from the Holy Bible, New International Version, copyright © 1973, 1978, 1984 International Bible Society. Used by permission of Zondervan Publishing House. All rights reserved.

    Scripture quotations marked TNIV are taken from the Holy Bible, Today's New International Version. Copyright © 2002 by International Bible Society. Used by permission of Hodder & Stoughton Publishers, A member of the Hodder Headline Group. All rights reserved. "TNIV" is a registered trademark of International Bible Society.

Library of Congress Cataloging-in-Publication Data
Simon, Arthur R.
Rediscovering the Lord's prayer / by Art Simon.
   p. cm.
Includes bibliographical references.
ISBN 0-8066-5134-2 (pbk. : alk. paper)
1. Lord's prayer. I. Title.
BV230.S444 2005
226.9'606—dc22   2004030283

Cover design by Diana Running, cover photo © Image Source/CORBIS. Used by permission.
Back cover author photo taken by Martin H. Simon. Used by permission.
Book design by Michelle L. N. Cook

The paper used in this publication meets the minimum requirements of American National Standard for Information Sciences—Permanence of Paper for Printed Library Materials, ANSI Z329.48-1984. ♾ ™

Manufactured in the U.S.A.

09   08   07   06   2   3   4   5   6   7   8   9   10

Royalties

All royalties for the sale of this book are being given to **Bread for the World,** a Christian citizens' movement that seeks justice for the world's hungry people by lobbying the nation's decision makers. For more information, contact:

Bread for the World
50 F. Street, N.W., Suite 500
Washington, D.C. 20001
Phone: 1-800-82BREAD or 1-800-822-7323
E-mail: bread@bread.org
Web site: www.bread.org

To my brother Paul,
servant of Christ
1928–2003

Table of Contents

Acknowledgments

I am indebted to many for help in the writing of this book, but I want to thank especially those who read my initial draft and offered comments that were exceptionally helpful. They include David Beckmann, Walter Boumann, Pat Brandenburg, Sarah Councell, Maynard Dorow, Paul Jersild, Mary C. McGuinness, O. P., Lloyd Neve, Harold Remus, and Kenneth Schwengel, In addition, William J. Byron, S. J., and Edward Simons helped on specific items. Dolly Youssef copied and mailed the manuscript to the readers and assisted in other ways.

I am deeply grateful to each of them. This book is much improved because of their help, though the deficiencies are mine. When I write, I do the best I can and offer the results, flaws and all, to God. The really nice thing about this is that God always receives it with a wonderful smile and puts it on the refrigerator.

Unless otherwise noted, I use the New Revised Standard Version when quoting from the Bible. Exceptions, noted in the text by abbreviations, include the King James Version (KJV), the New International Version (NIV), the Revised Standard Version (RSV), and Today's New International Version (TNIV).

1. A Confession

Let me tell you the unflattering truth. For most of my life I found the Lord's Prayer boring. Of course, that says much about me and nothing about the prayer. I grew up with it from infancy, and studied its petitions in confirmation class—first my own, later those I taught. I appreciated its theology, but praying it didn't especially move me.

The prayer seemed lifeless, perhaps in part because I prayed it mainly in church, where congregations run through it so fast that it's a done deal just when you get started. The words get said, but you hardly have time to think about what you are praying. It's like rushing through a museum or glancing for a split second at a spectacular sunset. Some things are meant to be soaked up, contemplated, savored, not just noticed.

Worse yet, the other main use of the Lord's Prayer in my experience was at church meetings when someone (often I) would say, "Let's close with the Lord's Prayer." And rattle it off we did. Like saluting the flag, we did it out of respect and habit, but not much thought— not mine at any rate. Meetings still close that way occasionally, and when they do, I grimace. But it seems more a violation of the commandment against a frivolous use of the Lord's name than heartfelt prayer. I speak for myself, not for those who focus more quickly and faithfully in the praying of this prayer.

Then my life was shaken to its roots by something I had always assumed would never happen to me, something that violated every bone in my Lutheran body. A divorce. My wife wanted out of the marriage. I'll say more about this later, but the point is that this personal adversity compelled me to pray as I had never prayed before. It made me think more deeply about many things I had taken for granted, including my truly desperate need of God. In the process I discovered the prayer of Jesus to be a hidden treasure.

The Lord's Prayer began to take on rich meaning for me in the face of crisis. It became a *door* that opened a way of coming to God for healing. I began to realize that the prayer has more to do with listening to God and living in God's presence than with speaking to God. It is more about purpose than about talk. The prayer now helps me want the right things and let God guide my life. This, I believe, is what Jesus intended when he presented the prayer to his disciples. He was not saying, "Look, boys, you can do this in twenty seconds," though he did tell them that piling up a lot of sanctimonious words is the wrong way to pray. Instead, in a few simple phrases he opened the way to a life of hope deeply rooted in God.

Many of you who read this may have discovered the riches of Jesus's prayer much earlier in life than I did and perhaps without need of a shaking. I do believe that the things of God, the essential things of life, are often grasped more quickly not by religious professionals, but by those with open hearts. Children. Poor people. Those who have suffered or learned from the suffering of others.

In this book I offer some personal reflections on the Lord's Prayer. It is not a scholarly analysis, but thoughts from a journey still in progress. I present the prayer the way I pray it, but if you prefer the traditional version or a more precise modern translation, that's perfectly fine. I usually pray it this way:

Our Father in heaven,
May Your holy name be honored.
Your kingdom come, your will be done
    on earth as in heaven.
Give us each day our daily bread.
Forgive us our sins
    as we forgive those who sin against us.
Lead us away from temptation,
    and deliver us from evil.
[For the kingdom, the power, and the glory are yours,
    now and forever. Amen.][1]

On the pages that follow I want to tell you as simply and clearly as I can how this prayer speaks to me, in the hope that it will enrich your life in God. Perhaps you too can rediscover its extraordinary power.

2. "Lord, Teach Us to Pray"

I take comfort in the fact that the disciples were also bumblers when it came to praying. They needed help, as all of us do. We are not alone in our difficulty; we are not the only ones who feel inadequate, because the right kind of praying does not come naturally to anyone. We instinctively want to get our way. We try to manipulate God and bargain with God for favors. We may use prayer as an escape hatch, resorting to it mainly when we fear some calamity. So it should not surprise us that we need to *learn* how to pray and what to pray for. That is why teaching children to pray when they are very young, and nourishing them in their praying, is essential so their life in God may grow deeper and richer.

Even if we have been taught to pray when we were young, most of us come to a point of time in adulthood when we realize how little we have grown in prayer, and how impoverished our prayer life is. We are tempted to give up. We may decide that we are not cut out to pray well. In any case, we are too busy; so praying gets pushed aside. I am appalled at how shallow and undisciplined my own praying was, even as a parish pastor deeply immersed in a fascinating inner city ministry. And I am embarrassed to say I didn't enjoy praying. I was aware of these deficiencies, but my feeble attempts to change never took hold. Each time, my praying would get sidetracked by the press of duties that I felt more competent to handle. Real or supposed urgencies replaced what was essential.

The disciples of Jesus sensed their poverty in prayer. Seeing Jesus pray led one of them to ask, "Lord, teach us to pray, as John taught his disciples" (Luke 11:1). They sought help, I believe, because they wanted a deeper relationship with God.

Their request, however, went far beyond that. In the Israel of Jesus's day each devout religious group would receive from its leader a special prayer (as the reference to John the Baptizer illustrates). That prayer gave the group a unique identity, reflected its mission, and bonded its members to the leader and to one another. The disciples of Jesus wanted that.

Jesus wanted it too, but he waited until they asked. And they asked because they saw what he was doing. Jesus did not give his disciples a model prayer so much as he *was* the model. The prayer bound them to him and included them in his unfolding mission. The Lord's Prayer still serves that purpose for us today, and all of Jesus's guidance regarding prayer should be understood in this light.

He encouraged his disciples to persist in prayer. Don't give up, he said, but keep on asking for what you need, because the Father delights in our coming and wants to give the best of gifts to those who ask (see Luke 11:5-13).

He urged them to avoid pretense. People who try to impress others when they pray, he said, are good actors, but terrible examples. So do not pray to be noticed, but pray in private where only God can see you and reward you (see Matthew 6:5-6).

Don't try to impress God, either, he advised. Babbling on and on in prayer, he said, is a waste of time, because the Father knows what we need before we ask (Matthew 6:7-8). And do not boast of your accomplishments. Simply offer yourself to God. Lay out your sins honestly, as did the tax collector, and ask God to forgive you. No pretense needed and no pretense allowed, said Jesus. Come just as you are (see Luke 18:10-14).

We can take much comfort from all of this. When I told several friends that I was writing some reflections on prayer, one said, "I don't know how to say the right words." Another told me, "I have always prayed but have not developed words suitable for God." Ironically, both pray in a way that is beautiful in its simplicity and love.

Walter Wangerin Jr., pastor and author, confirms these virtues from his own experience:

> Once early in our marriage, Thanne demanded that we pray out loud together. I was a student at the seminary, yet prayer embarrassed me. So we went into the bedroom, turned out the lights, lay down on our backs—and I started. I prayed in big words with heavy cadences, like a hymnal. When I was done, I congratulated myself on a job well done.
>
> But then Thanne's voice arose in the darkness, softly talking to God as if they were alone and I was an eavesdropper.
>
> And she named my name! Not to me, but to God she said "Wally" with such love and gentleness that I began to cry. In the private precincts of prayer Thanne's love became a holy thing. It brought the breathing of the Spirit down upon my silly soul, and I cried.[1]

*   *   *   *

Jesus not only gives us the right words, he also lets us know that the right words are those that come from the heart. These may be expressed in psalms or hymns, or in our own stumbling speech. No special vocabulary needed, no fancy language required. Spareness and sincerity will do just fine. Often no words are needed at all—just a smile, a hug, perhaps tears, or simply the desire to be in God's presence.

Or the prayer of our Lord.

A friend of mine, grief-stricken when her son was killed, told me that when she could find no words of her own to bring to God, the prayer of Jesus was a gift that carried her. She mentioned the value of its familiarity. "When life gets tough, it comes to mind," she said. In a similar way, when I needed it most, the prayer came to mind like a neglected investment that had accumulated surprising capital. If there are "sighs too deep for words" in prayer (Romans 8:26), there are also words too deep for sighs—words that carry us forward when we cannot adequately frame our own. The prayer of Jesus does this for us.

> Lord, draw us closer to you.
> Help us to listen,
> that your purpose for us
> may become our own.

There is much more to prayer than our words and our sighs. Mother Teresa was once asked what she did when she prayed. "I listen," she responded.[2] What we know of Jesus's prayer life, along with the content of the Lord's Prayer, leads me to conclude that he is not just giving us a string of petitions, but inviting us to listen to God, to reflect on God's will for us, to become more aware of God's presence and more attuned to our mission in life. The prayer is not about how we can influence God, but about entering the heart of God and letting God lead us. That requires listening.

Jesus withdrew from the disciples and the crowds on occasion to pray privately; and before choosing his twelve disciples he spent an entire night in prayer (Luke 6:12). Because Jesus warned against the use of too many words, it is hard to imagine his praying as a monologue. He must have been listening intently, seeking his Father's will.

It is in such seeking that we let the prayer of Jesus guide our thoughts and desires as well as the words that we bring to God. Dialogue.

It may seem a contradiction that Jesus frames his prayer as a prayer for the entire group of disciples, yet advises them to pray in private. He intended both. Private praying was urged in contrast to showing off in public, not as a substitute for prayer in temple, synagogue, and home. As the defining prayer for his followers, the Lord's Prayer was used by believers from the earliest days of the church, especially when Christians gathered to celebrate Holy Communion.

Prayers with fellow believers and our private prayers interact, which is why even the much-too-hurried praying of the Lord's Prayer in church plays an essential role in keeping this prayer alive. The private praying of it gives us time to listen and reflect. This enriches our praying with others. Corporate prayer in turn nourishes our private prayers and often carries us through periods when our private praying seems a wasteland.

When our prayer life becomes feeble or barren, may that not reveal a need to renew a relationship of love with God? Paul Tournier, the Swiss psychologist, tells of a husband and wife who rarely spoke to each other. "There's nothing to talk about," one of them explained. What does it mean when we feel we have nothing much to discuss with God? Does that not indicate an impoverishment of spirit and the need to seek God's grace?

Relationships take time and effort, of course. What motivates us to make that effort may be a feeling of emptiness or the realization that there is more to life than we now experience. Whatever our situation, we can begin with God's great love for us in Christ. We can remember who we are—we who have been baptized into his name. We can remember that God has given us a purpose in Christ, a mission to accomplish during our few short years on earth. Then we can—ever so slowly—use the words of Jesus's prayer to open conversation with God, listen to God, and think about our life in relation to God. There will soon be much to talk about.

ur

..nity.

. Prayer boring because my

. I missed the intensity of its

: lens of a lesser reality?

In praying this prayer we enter a new dimension of life where God rules and pure love prevails. We put ourselves consciously within God's kingdom because it is our true home, even in this world of sin and death. Opening our hearts and minds to God allows us to taste life as it was meant to be, as we long for it to be, as it one day will be, and as we can begin to practice it now. Far from suggesting an escape from the nitty-gritty of this life, the prayer of Jesus addresses it head-on. But the prayer always ties our present life to the future, because it is based on hope in Christ and his kingdom. It empowers us to live more fully in the present, while it carries us forward to that day when Christ returns in glory and the entire prayer will be completely answered.

Nowhere in the four gospels does Jesus define prayer. He does not define the kingdom of God either, but instead conveys in stories and metaphors what it is like. The same is true of prayer, because there is mystery in prayer, just as there is mystery in life itself and in the kingdom of God. They encompass more than our human understanding can receive. Jesus does not explain away the mystery. Instead he reveals to us the heart and soul of prayer, which is to put our life more completely into God's hands—trust seeking more trust.

3. Our Father in Heaven

What seems to us a commonplace beginning of Jesus's prayer was anything but that to the people of Judea. Depicting God as Father was rare, though not unknown in the Old Testament. "As a father has compassion for his children, so the LORD has compassion for those who fear him," the psalmist assures us in the grandest of psalms (Psalm 103:13). But Jesus spoke of God as *his* Father. He asserted a relationship with God that was intimate and special. In giving this prayer to his followers as their identifying prayer, and opening it with the words, "Our Father," Jesus was inviting us to share in this same intimate relationship. We pray to the Father through Jesus. Because of Jesus we are no longer orphans, but children of God.

Jesus almost certainly used *Abba*, the word for "Father" in the Aramaic language that he spoke. It is a term of childlike endearment. *Abba* must have been invented by babies when they were uttering their first words. Similar sounds are first words in many cultures and languages. You can visualize a ten-month-old infant smiling and reaching toward her father and calling out, "Ab-ba! Ab-ba!" You can also imagine her father's face beaming as he picks her up and holds her in his arms. The joy, the love, and the privilege for both are palpable. That is exactly God's desire for us, nothing less than that we love him and reach out to him as our *Abba* in our utter dependence and with our love.

I am tempted to translate it "Daddy" because that would capture some of its intimacy; but Daddy is too casual. To the fearful and disheartened, however, the assurance that we can come to God as confidently as children run to their dear father is the sweetest of good news.

The New Testament was written in Greek, the international language of the Roman Empire, some years after Jesus's earthly life. So *Abba* was translated with the Greek word for father. But the Gospel of Mark (14:36) inserts *Abba* before "Father" in the Greek text when Jesus prays in the Garden of Gethsemane, and the apostle Paul does the same in two of his letters (Romans 8:15; Galatians 4:6). This gave it particular emphasis, like a flag saying, "The God and Father of Jesus is not distant and aloof. He is our own dear Father!"

The beauty of it is that our *Abba* delights in our coming to him no matter how halting our words or imperfect our expressions of love. We are like a four-year-old, drawing a picture and offering it to her daddy. "Beautiful!" the father announces. With the same delight God also accepts the flawed offerings of our lives. "Beautiful!" says God, who sees not the flaws but the love, made perfect in Christ, that lies behind them.[1]

Paul's use of *Abba* is especially instructive. It indicates that from the earliest days of the church, "*Abba*, Father!" has become widely used. So Paul can remind the Christians of Rome and Galatia of something they already knew—that the Holy Spirit, persuades us that we are children of God, enables us to cry, *a*, Father!" Paul says that as children of our *Abba*, we are s with Christ of a promised glory. We look to the day when God will complete the redemption of our bodies and of the whole creation (see Romans 8:14-25). In short, the words "Our Father" are packed not simply with intimacy, but with expectation. They underscore the way in which the prayer of Jesus reaches toward the future. The kingdom, here now in Jesus but still to be unfolded in all of its splendor, is like a powerful electric current that runs through the entire prayer, and it begins with the words, "Our Father." God was a father to Israel when rescuing the Hebrews from slavery (see Exodus 4:22-23), and Jesus fulfilled the mission of Israel. By inviting us to call God our Father he is asking us to join him in a new Exodus, a journey with him through this earthly wilderness into the promised land of God's everlasting reign.[2]

People have often wondered why this prayer, as it appears in Matthew 6:9-13 and Luke 11:2-4, contains no line of praise or thanksgiving. But as the first two words so brilliantly illustrate, the entire prayer exudes praise and thanksgiving. For what could be more pleasing to a father than having his own little child climb on his lap and hug him and call him "Daddy"? That is high praise. The psalmist knew this when he wrote, "O LORD, our Lord, how majestic is thy name in all the earth! Thou whose glory above the heavens is chanted by the mouth of babes and infants" (Psalm 8:1-2 RSV).

Our *Abba* in heaven is spirit, so we cannot literally sit on his lap or hug him. But that does not mean he is far away, either, for God is everywhere; and heaven is where God's gracious reign is fully realized. So God is closer to us than we are to ourselves, for "in him we live and move and have our being" (Acts 17: 28). We show our affection to God by our love and trust, and in the praise that flows to God from our hearts; and we show it especially in the way we treat others and the rest of God's creation.

We know God as our Father through Jesus, who was sent to reveal the Father's love, a love that endured even the horror of the cross. There Jesus showed the depth of God's longing for us, and there he offered his life as a sacrifice for our sins and for those of the whole world. It was God's own sacrifice. In Jesus God was reconciling lost and alienated children to himself. So the Father whom we call upon in prayer is the Father who has called us first, the Father who created us and then brought us home again through Jesus when we were lost.

Many people understand Jesus and the Father in a very different way. They have been taught to think of God the Father as an angry judge who is so offended at human rebellion that he is determined to send us all into the everlasting flames of hell. God the Son, however, is so compassionate that he placates the Father's anger by coming to earth and suffering that punishment for us. But this understanding of God as split personalities misses the whole point. "*God* so loved the world that he gave his only Son" (John 3:16), and "in Christ *God* was reconciling the world to himself" (2 Corinthians 5:19). In Jesus *God* took the punishment for our sins on the cross. So Jesus wants us to know that the Father is not a vindictive, angry scold, but our *Abba*. Jesus showed us how much the Father loves us. And on the cross he provided the way to our Father through the grace of forgiveness, which the Father delights to give. "See what great love *the Father* has lavished on us, that we should be called children of God!" (1 John 3:1 TNIV).

It is easy, of course, to talk in glowing terms about God's love. Believing it may seem absurd, however, considering the dark side of God's creation. Suffering and injustice make life for many a living hell. Jesus reached out with special intention to such people. He identified with them. And as the cross tells us, God is not removed from the suffering of his children. Nor should we be. Our compassion, shown in works of mercy and justice, is the most convincing evidence of that love.

God and Gender

Today many object to the name *Father,* which seems to stereotype God as male. I sympathize with those who feel this discomfort. The name is so deeply anchored in the faith of Jesus, however, that we rightly address God as the Father, Son, and Holy Spirit into whom we were baptized. That does not indicate a gender bias, however. The Bible also compares God to a mother. "As a mother comforts her child, so I will comfort you" (Isaiah 66:13). And when Jesus approached Jerusalem for the last time, weeping as he looked upon the city, he said, "Jerusalem, Jerusalem . . . How often have I desired to gather your children together as a hen gathers her brood under her wings, and you were not willing" (Luke 13:34). Furthermore, the creation account not only says that "God created humankind in his image," but adds, "male *and female*" he created them" (Genesis 1:27). Both genders reflect the image of God.

> Thank you, Abba, for adopting us in love through your son Jesus. Be patient with us as we try to imitate you, because we are such slow learners.

Some people have not experienced the love of an earthly father, or have experienced it in a way that leaves them conflicted. Perhaps the father abused them sexually, or was remote and lacking in affection. Or perhaps he abandoned them and left them with a life-long emptiness, so they have no feeling at all toward him or only deep resentment. In such cases, to think of God as Father may seem to be a hindrance rather than a help. My father was the most compassionate man I ever knew, so I can only imagine what those with opposite experiences may feel.

Some who had miserable or absent parents tell me that they find great comfort and joy in having a heavenly Father whose love for them far exceeds everything they missed from their earthly mother or father. My own mother was abandoned as an infant, and her adoptive parents died when she was only a few years old. She was taken in by an elderly aunt with severe emotional problems who resented the unexpected burden of raising a young child—and she let my mother know it. So Mom had painful memories from her childhood. She often said that except for the great love she felt from God, she would not have survived.

For many the pain from childhood is not easily erased. The intention of Jesus, in any case, is clear: to let us know that God, our Father through Jesus, is a Father who loves us far more than any earthly parent ever has or ever could.

Relationship

I think one of the great gifts of parenthood is that, through our own joy and heartache, we get a glimpse of God. My children have given me incredible joy. But if one of them becomes troubled or distant even for a while, or wanders from the path of life in Christ, that becomes a sorrow, precisely because I love them so much. Then it occurs to me that God feels exactly the same way about us, only more so. I think how poorly I have treated God—seldom listening to God and largely ignoring God's presence. I've taken blessings for granted, complained when I should have been praising, treated God as an outsider, an uninvited guest. All this despite the goodness that God, so patient, so forgiving, continues to offer.

In addressing God as our Father, Jesus is reminding us how much we mean to God. He is calling us to a new relationship with the One who created us, who knows us completely and whose image we bear. The Hebrew word for *knowing* God, and for God *knowing* us, is the same as the word for sexual intercourse. Adam "*knew* his wife Eve, and she conceived" (Genesis 4:1). We learn from this that knowing God—yes, calling God our *Abba*—is no formality, like approaching a lofty dignitary with "Sir" or "Your

Honor" or "Mr. President." Rather it is that hug, that beaming face from the one who loves us more deeply than we love ourselves, and on whom our life depends.

"Our Father" signals an intimate relationship with others as well as with God. The Father to whom we belong is also the Father of others. That's why the Lord's Prayer begins "*Our* Father," not just *my* Father. We have many brothers and sisters. We know only a small number of them, and we probably do not like some of them. But we have the same heavenly Father, who loves them as deeply as he loves us, and who calls us to love them also, for "everyone who loves the parent loves the child" (1 John 5:1). "The commandment we have from him is this: those who love God must love their brothers and sisters also" (1 John 4:21).

As a boy, when I complained to my father about someone and told him I didn't feel like being nice to that person, he would suggest, "If you can't do it for Johnny, why don't you do it for God?" Then he would remind me of God's love in a way that would melt my heart and make it seem like being nice to Johnny was a special way of thanking God, which it was.

"Therefore be imitators of God, as beloved children," we are urged, "and live in love, as Christ loved us and gave himself up for us, a fragrant offering and sacrifice to God" (Ephesians 5:1-2). In approaching God as our Father, we are not only warmly received, but warmly reminded that our purpose in life is to reflect what God is like. Because my earthly father was so good to me, I loved him dearly and *wanted* to be like him. Should we not be even more eager to imitate and please our beloved *Abba?*

If *knowing* is the word for physical intimacy and bringing new life into the world, then knowing God as our Father must be a relationship that is life-giving and fruitful, one in which we reproduce (however imperfectly) the love that God has for each member of the human family. We learn this from the Hebrew Scriptures and, most of all, from Jesus himself.

In his book, *Credo*, assembled as he inched toward death, William Sloane Coffin wrote:

> When Jesus says, "Our Father, who art in heaven," I listen. Even during my doubting days in college I listened, and carefully, because Jesus knew not only more about God than I did—that was obvious; he also knew more about the world. He could talk convincingly to me about a father in heaven because he took seriously the earth's homeless orphans. He could talk to me convincingly about living at peace in the hands of love because he knew that the world lived constantly at war in the grip of hatred. He could talk to me of light, and joy, and exultation, because I knew that he himself knew darkness, sorrow, and death. That's why, eventually, Jesus became for me too my Lord and Savior, and that's why I think it right to say that the authority of the Lord's Prayer stems from the reliability of the source.[3]

The treasured words, "Our Father," draw us into themes that recur throughout the prayer of Jesus. They address our present condition while always pointing beyond it to the time when our status as children of the kingdom will be fully revealed. They play, as do the petitions that follow, like variations of a symphonic melody. Together they overlap and interweave with one another to create a magnificent tapestry of devotion and hope. Two simple words, "Our Father," celebrate the goodness of God and lift us above our human failure. They put us in God's hands where we belong so that we become more fully alive.

4. May Your Holy Name Be Honored

One's name is of priceless value. Ruin your reputation, and your name—your life—is burdened with a debt of dishonor. The names Abraham Lincoln and Adolph Hitler evoke polar opposite reactions because of what each did. Companies spend fortunes to present a favorable name to the public.

God's name is also of priceless value—priceless beyond compare—and God cares deeply about protecting that great and holy name. We should too, if God is the one we truly love and trust above all else.

In this petition we exclaim how holy the Father's name is and how much we want it honored. We anticipate the time when the whole creation will honor the Father's name and give it undiluted praise.[1] Meanwhile we begin to do so now, in a world in which the honor of that name is obscured by sin and unbelief.

Jesus here takes the commandment, "You shall not misuse the name of the LORD your God" (Exodus 20:7 NIV), and moves a giant step beyond it. The commandment tells us what *not* to do, but this petition tells us what to *aspire* to do. The prohibition is transformed into an opportunity that embraces the commandment while opening our hearts to seek its fulfillment in praise and deeds of love.

"Your holy name be honored," we pray. May the whole world, the whole creation sing your praise. May it reflect the peace, the love, and the justice of your kingdom, starting with us. Now.

"God's name is indeed holy in itself, but we pray in this petition that it may be holy among us also," wrote Martin Luther in his *Small Catechism*.

But *how* do we honor God's holy name?

We do so by our speech. Even more by our behavior.

Speech

We honor God's holy name by lifting up our hearts in prayer, praise, and thanksgiving to the Father for loving us so deeply in Christ and filling us with hope. We honor that name by faithfully hearing God's Word and sharing it with others. We honor it by speaking truthfully, defending those who are being put down or oppressed, offering encouragement to the disheartened, and by reflecting God's love in kind and friendly words. *Everything* we say or refrain from saying, even our unspoken thoughts and desires, should honor God.

By the same measure we dishonor God's name by using it wrongfully, speaking lovelessly, or harboring loveless desires.

Since long before Christ, devout Jews have fastidiously sought to avoid abusing God's name by never uttering the word *Yahweh*—the name by which God was revealed to Moses and the Israelites as the God who made a covenant of love with them. When scribes copied the Hebrew Scriptures, *Yahweh* was marked with vowels for the word *adonai* ("the Lord"), warning the reader to say *adonai* rather than *Yahweh*. "The LORD" is still printed in English translations with "ORD" in small capital letters to indicate that it stands for the Hebrew *Yahweh*. And to this day observant Jews do not say or write *Yahweh*. In this way they exercise extreme care never to take the name of God in vain.

You may question whether such precaution was what God had in mind with the second commandment (or third, as some number it). But you have to admire the respect that lies behind such determination, standing as it does in stark contrast to the careless and manipulative use of God's name that has become so common today. I think it is fair to say that our language reflects a cultural shift over the last few decades of "defining deviancy downward," as yesterday's off-limits profanity has become today's acceptable speech.

To cite one small example, the expression "O my God!" is standard fare on just about every television sit-com, a fact that is both cause and consequence of its widespread use and acceptance in everyday speech. "But I don't mean anything by it," I have heard people say. Precisely the point. Using God's name when you don't mean anything by it cheapens respect for the one who has loved us above all others—a poor way to treat any friend, much less our beloved *Abba*.

It doesn't take much to pull us down. Growing up in western Oregon, I attended an eight-grade public school where cursing was almost never heard. Then one year a few big kids who were "cussers" transferred in. Soon most of the other older boys and quite a few younger ones began to cuss—and, oh, how I felt like cussing too! I came within a razor's edge of caving in. So quickly does the culture change, and so easily do we change with it.

When Sarah Councell, a bright young staff member of Bread for the World, read the above paragraph in the first draft of this book, she commented, "This example will ring true for many older readers. Younger ones may not quite be able to believe it meant so much, which exactly proves your point. Profanity just doesn't seem like a big deal."

Obscenities also dishonor God. People use gutter language to project an image of toughness, imagining that it strengthens their speech when it merely reveals their location. Speech that belittles others, racial or ethnic slurs, vicious or innocent gossip (now there's an oxymoron!), a complaining, judgmental tongue, or simply words spoken in a way that reflects indifference toward others—these betray a lovelessness that brings no honor to God, especially from the lips of a believer.

We may also dishonor God by our silence. We may fail to speak up for those who are poor and hungry, racially different, or ridiculed and mistreated for some other reason; or we may keep quiet when those around us applaud a way of life that we know to be morally destructive. We honor God by putting in a word for the gift of grace that

> *Oh, Father, may our love for you become so deep and true, that we will honor your holy name in all we think and say, in all we desire and do.*

we have received from the Father. But we dishonor God by being pushy, arrogant, or foolhardy in our witness; or by saying nothing when we have opportunity to share the hope that is within us. There is no easy formula here, other than seeking always to speak the truth in love. In this petition we pray for the wisdom and grace to do so.

Perhaps the most serious dishonoring of God's name in speech is using it to manipulate others. One way is invoking God's name to deceive others. Another is attending church or mouthing religious sentiments to impress others, for we then worship ourselves rather than God. I know how easy it is, as a pastor, to care more about making a good impression than nourishing the flock. The line distinguishing the two can be very thin.

God's name is often harnessed for political purposes. A candidate for public office may do so to win support from voters. Citizens may assume that God is on our nation's side in every war and every international dispute, but such arrogance dishonors both nation and God. There are too many examples in our own country and other countries of people demeaning, brutalizing, or killing others in the name of God, a travesty against the Father who created each one of us in his image. This is a special danger in time of war, when presidents and pastors readily invoke God's name to rally national support and assure us of our own righteousness.

How different the understanding of Lincoln, who in the middle of the nation's bloodiest conflict proclaimed a national day of fasting (March 30, 1863) by saying,

> We have grown in numbers, wealth, and power, as no other nation has ever grown. But we have forgotten God. We have forgotten the gracious hand which preserved us in peace, and multiplied and enriched and strengthened us; and we have vainly imagined, in the deceitfulness of our hearts, that all these blessings were produced by some superior wisdom and virtue of our own. Intoxicated with unbroken success, we have become too self-sufficient to feel the necessity of redeeming and preserving grace, too proud to pray to the God that made us.

In his second inaugural address near the end of that war, Lincoln did not boast of the North's impending victory, but saw in the conflict the judgment of God against the nation as a whole for allowing slavery. Urging "malice toward none [and] charity for all," he called upon citizens North and South "to bind up the nation's wounds, to care for him who shall have borne the battle and for his widow and his orphan."

How we speak reflects who we are and what we believe. If we are children of the kingdom, even the tone of a simple "Good morning!" inescapably casts a reflection on God in the eyes of others. I often forget that, but the prayer of Jesus reminds me.

Behavior

The line between speech and behavior is inexact, because speech is also a form of behavior and behavior a form of communication. When Jesus urged his followers to be truth-tellers whose word could always be trusted with a simple "Yes" or "No," he was demanding a level of honesty that rules out any deception, any cheating in the conduct of business or in dealings of any kind. Speech and behavior interlock.

But if we distinguish between speech and behavior, it must be said that behavior is the more important of the two. We usually bring more honor or dishonor to God by what we do or fail to do than by what we say or fail to say. "Actions speak louder than words." This may mean changing what we do, but it may also mean changing the way we do it—"doing for God what we ordinarily do for ourselves," as Brother Lawrence put it.[2]

In the Sermon on the Mount, following the beatitudes, Jesus said, "Let your light shine before others, so they may see your good works and give glory to your Father in heaven" (Matthew 5:16).[3] The doing of good, more than anything else, should enable others to see in us a reflection of the face of God.

The reverse is also true. If we do evil, or if our light does not shine because we fail to do good, we disgrace the Father. The prophets deplored and the apostle Paul echoed that the name of God is widely blasphemed by nonbelievers because of the behavior of believers (see Romans 2:24). And the psalmist prayed, "Do not let those who hope in you be put to shame because of me" (Psalm 69:6).

Clarence Jordan founded the inter-racial Koinonia community in Georgia during the days when segregation was strictly observed in the Bible Belt, and the Ku Klux Klan terrorized people and sometimes lynched black people to enforce it. Jordan said, "You don't take the name of the Lord in vain with your lips. You take it in vain with your life. It isn't the people outside the church who take God's name in vain. It's the people on the inside, the nice people who would never dare let one little cuss word fall off their lips—they're the ones many times whose lives are totally unchanged by the grace of God."[4]

I think Jordan overstated in saying you don't misuse the Lord's name with your lips; but his emphasis on the importance of living in a way that matches the faith we confess is on target. Writer and popular scholar, Tony Campolo, was talking about poverty and faith in a university chapel service, but the students seemed bored. Some were dozing. Out of exasperation he blurted, "Thirty thousand children are dying needlessly every day of hunger or diseases related to hunger in developing countries, and you don't give a damn!" That got everybody's attention. Tony continued, "And you are more shocked that I used the word 'damn' in chapel than that thousands of children are needlessly dying. That's what's wrong with our Christianity. We are more concerned about people using four letter words than we are with the fact that our hearts are not broken by the things that break the heart of Jesus."[5]

May the light of Christ shine so brightly in us that others will see the good that we do and give glory to you, Father.

As for Jordan, during a boycott by the white establishment against the Koinonia Farm to try to drive them from the county, he went into town to buy a sack of chicken feed. The man behind the counter flushed with anger and ordered him to get out of the store. As Jordan was leaving, the man yelled to him that if he and the Koinonia people would run an ad in the local paper renouncing integration, he would sell him anything he wanted. Jordan stopped, slowly walked back to the counter. "Excuse me, sir," he said quietly. "I came in here this morning simply to buy a sack of feed. I didn't come in to sell my soul."[6]

Stephen Carter, professor of law at Yale University, cites a survey showing that 70 percent of college students admit to having cheated on a test. He says: "we shouldn't be surprised, because that is what we teach, that what really matters is getting grades, getting the test results, getting the car, getting the big house, etc. And with some exceptions, most Americans who call themselves religious are participating in this rush toward material goodies just as hard as everybody else in the culture." He adds that politicians often say, in effect, "I'm a religious person too, though my policies are actually aimed at advancing this materialistic, careerist battle further."[7] So folks draw on religion to support rather than critique a culture that in many respects is hostile to the biblical witness. Consider the extent to which even the pulpits of our churches have become a chaplaincy for the culture of affluence, assenting to it mostly by silence. To the extent that this is true it discredits the name of God.

Following my father's example, my brother Paul devoted his life with exceptional intensity to helping others, both personally and in public office. He loved people. His idea of a really good time was getting to know the janitor, the immigrant cleaning lady, and the cashier. He cared about the woman without dentures, the family without food, the prisoner, the child mentally or physically challenged, the man who couldn't read; and he spent his adult life pursuing justice for them. He was buried on the anniversary of his baptism. Seventy-five years earlier, to the day, Paul had been buried with Christ by baptism into his death, and rose with Christ to a new life. It was in that life that Paul tried to be faithful. He was careful not to parade his faith, but many throughout the state of Illinois and beyond were aware of it. Paul wanted his life, however imperfectly, to honor God.

Dianne Coluccio is a young member of the Pro Sanctity Movement, a movement within the Roman Catholic Church that encourages people to holiness of life in mind, heart, and hands (theology, spirituality, and service). She and other young members decided to volunteer at a soup kitchen in Brooklyn. In her words, after hours of spirited work in the kitchen:

> the guests came through the doors—cold, wet, old, young, men, women, families. They came clutching whatever they had—for some it was only a coat. Still others had shopping bags that perhaps held everything they owned. Many looked through a rack of used clothing, and we watched their faces light up when they found that one special piece. I found myself saying a short silent prayer, "God, forgive me for running to Macy's to buy that Ralph Lauren sweater that we both know I didn't need." God's presence was strong and our need to be there apparent. The place was packed and this acted as a wake-up call for all of us."[8]

She wrote more, but you get the idea.

The honoring of God's name is not just a matter of personal acts of love. It involves public justice as well. The prophet Amos records the Lord's anger against Israel because the people were profaning God's holy name by their idolatry and sexual immorality, but most of all by their injustice toward poor people (Amos 2:6-8). As a result, God rejected their worship:

I hate, I despise your festivals,
>   and I take no delight in your solemn assemblies.
Take away from me the noise of your songs;
>   I will not listen to the melody of your harps.
But let justice roll down like waters,
>   and righteousness like an everflowing stream
(Amos 5:21, 23-24).

In the priestly tradition of Leviticus, the Israelites were forbidden to eat unclean creatures, part of the ritual for holiness. God gave them a reason for their pursuit of holiness: "I am the LORD who brought you up out of Egypt to be your God; therefore be holy, because I am holy" (Leviticus 11:45 NIV). God's holiness is seen in the rescue of the enslaved people of Israel, a monumental act of justice. The Israelites are therefore to be holy also—called to pursue justice for others. Pursuing justice was not to be done instead of religious ritual, but it was to be consistent with it.

As a child, Alice Gahana survived two concentration camps during the Holocaust. Asked what she remembered most, she replied, "The empty windows." German soldiers came to her little village when she was nine years old and told her family to come to the village square:

> I walked that morning carrying my suitcase, down our cobble-stoned street—the street that I had walked all my life, by houses in which lived people I had known all my life. . . . But as I walked down the street, I noticed the windows were empty. No one came to the windows. My friends and neighbors knew what was happening, they knew—but they were afraid. Nobody came to the windows to see what was happening to me.[9]

Her story described the failure of personal compassion, but that failure is tied immediately to a grave public injustice, an injustice that was able to flourish because millions of nominal Christians failed to demonstrate compassion. Alice Gahana must have wondered, "What kind of God do they believe in?"

Senator Joseph Lieberman is an observant Orthodox Jew. A favorite phrase of his is *kiddush Hashem,* "sanctifying God's name through one's actions," which for Lieberman means that he sees his faith guiding his politics.[10] There are both bad and good ways of doing that, but the underlying principle holds, that faith is to inform and shape the whole of our life, not just selected parts of it.

We honor God's holy name with a holy life. Not that we can be sinless, but that we live as forgiven sinners, set apart by God for a special purpose. So the praying of this petition invites personal inventory. How are we honoring or dishonoring that good and holy name? What are we saying or not saying, doing or failing to do? How do we relate to others? How can we better reflect the hope that has drawn us into the Father's kingdom?

You may have more suitable questions for yourself. Whatever the path of our reflection, the destination we aspire to is joy in bringing honor to God in all that we say, do, and desire, eagerly awaiting the day when honor to that holy name "will blaze out in ways that all must acknowledge."[11]

5. Your Kingdom Come

When I was a young boy I had terrible
vision and didn't know it. I remember
being embarrassed as a second grader
when the teacher made me take a seat in
the front row so I could read what was on
the blackboard; but strangely, neither the
teacher nor I thought to report this to my
parents. Then the following summer an
eye examination revealed that I was badly
nearsighted and needed glasses. When I
put my new glasses on, I was astonished
to see my surroundings in focus for the
first time. Faces were no longer blurry. I
could distinguish distant leaves and individual blades of grass. The world had
not changed, but my ability to see it sure
had.

The kingdom of God is like that.
It brings us an astonishing new view of
reality. The world does not change, but
we see it in a different way, as it truly is,
through the eyes of God. We begin to see

ourselves, and others, and all things that way. The love and purpose of God come into focus for us. We no longer understand life apart from Christ but through Christ. We look at everything in a different way because we see it through the lens of the kingdom. Such vision is a gift that God eagerly wants us to have because he loves us so very much.

Being a father to four children has helped me understand God's deep love for us. Parents often want more for their children than the children want for themselves. It shows up in simple instructions such as, "Eat your vegetables," or "Tell Susan you're sorry." Our children may behave foolishly, while we want them to live wisely. They may abandon the faith of their baptism, while we shed tears and pray for their return.

Like the most devoted parent you can imagine, our *Abba* has great dreams and plans for his children. He wants much more for us than we want for ourselves. *Our problem is not that we desire too much, but that we desire too little.* We may spend our lives chasing affluence and pursuing happiness, but the Father wants us to follow Jesus. We may try to squeeze what we can for ourselves out of this short life, but God offers us a purpose in life that is far more challenging and rewarding. We are like a prisoner on death row who dreams of a steak dinner for his last meal, while God wants to set us free.

God longs to give us an everlasting kingdom. God is eager for us to let go of lesser attractions and participate fully in life with the risen Christ, which begins now and never ends.

From beginning to end, the Lord's Prayer is a prayer of and for the kingdom, a prayer that the compassionate and powerful reign of God would come. It is also a prayer that God's will, not our own, be done. These are not so much two separate petitions—although we usually treat them as such—but one petition that is made and then repeated. The ancient Hebrews liked to say something and then say it again in a different way to give it emphasis and to enrich its meaning. We have many instances of this in the Bible. For example:

Create in me a clean heart, O God,
     and put a new and right spirit within me
(Psalm 51:10).

But let justice roll down like waters,
     and righteousness like an everflowing stream
(Amos 5:24).

"Your kingdom come, your will be done," is another such instance. To pray for the coming of the kingdom is to pray for God's will to be accomplished; and to pray that God's will be done is to pray that God would govern our lives more completely. Yet each has a distinct emphasis. "Your kingdom come" reminds us that our hope reaches into the future, while "Your will be done" focuses on living in the kingdom now.

Jesus and the Kingdom

"The time is fulfilled, and the kingdom of God has come near; repent, and believe in the good news" (Mark 1:15), Jesus announced. In today's language he might have said, "The promised time has come. God is about to reclaim this fallen world. Open your heart to this good news and give your life to God."

Jesus was distilling the message of the Hebrew prophets who had envisioned a time when God would come to rescue his people from captivity, dwell with them, rule over them, make a new and everlasting covenant with them, and remember their sins no more. God, they said, would rule with compassion and justice, and with the care of a shepherd. The vision was often intertwined with the promise of a Messiah-king and even a Messiah-servant who would suffer and die for the sins of the people.

Jesus knew these prophecies well and embodied them in his own mission. By his words and actions he made clear that God's time had come, and these promises were being fulfilled in his own person. It was an astonishing claim.

So when Jesus told his disciples to pray, "Your kingdom come," he was asking them to pray that his mission, dangerous and uncertain,[1] might be accomplished. And it *was* accomplished, though not at all in the way they expected. First they were crushed by Jesus's crucifixion. Then his resurrection turned their despair to joy and, through the Holy Spirit, fired them with hope. The kingdom *had* come in Jesus and would, some day soon they thought, be revealed in great splendor. They had a Savior and Lord. They had a mission. They now saw life through the new lens of the kingdom.

> *Father, give us eyes to see that we are participants now in your everlasting kingdom*

For us to pray "Your kingdom come" is to be fired with the same hope and to see life through the same lens—or at least to ask for such fire and such vision, when we do not have it.

Helen Crane remembers when this vision suddenly became clear to her. She was in the fifth grade, and the teacher was explaining the different biological kingdoms. The teacher asked the girl sitting next to Helen, "What kingdom do you belong to?" The girl paused for moment and then replied, "I belong to the kingdom of God." The teacher ran out of the room crying. "I am eighty-six years old, and I still recall that moment as if it happened today," she said.[2]

When Jesus spoke of the kingdom, he told stories and used metaphors. It is like a farmer planting seeds in his field and waiting for the harvest. It is like a grain of mustard seed, the tiniest of seeds, but when it takes root and grows it becomes a shrub so large that the birds build nests in its branches. It is like a treasure so valuable that a person sells everything he has to buy the field in which it is hidden in order to claim the treasure (see Matthew 13:24-32, 44).

Christians sometimes talk about "building" the kingdom, but this modern expression would have seemed strangely out of place to Jesus. His images of the kingdom had to do with the mystery of life. The kingdom is not something we construct; it is a work of God's power and love.

The word *kingdom* suggests to us a country or region with political boundaries. That misleads. The word, both in the Aramaic language that Jesus used and in the Greek New Testament, means king*ship*. It refers to the ruling or reigning activity of God in rescuing people from sin and death, and bringing about a new creation. We don't build it or make it happen. It is all God's doing, God's extraordinary work. The kingdom *comes*. It comes to us from God in the person of Jesus, in our daily lives. It is at once God's gift of love and a call to action.

Our prayer does not make the kingdom come. Nevertheless, Jesus wants us to pray, and pray fervently, that it may come to us now, in this world of sin, where we receive it and celebrate it imperfectly by faith. And he wants us to long for the day when the reign of God will be revealed in its glory.

We want God to rule more fully in our own lives, but we want that for others as well. "If we genuinely love people, we desire for them far more than it is within our power to give, and that will cause us to pray," writes Richard Foster.[3] So in this petition we pray that others too may discover the reign of God through faith in Jesus, seek it more than anything else, and finally enjoy its fullness in the resurrection. That makes it a prayer for our sisters and brothers in Christ, as well as a prayer for the mission of the church in drawing others to Christ. We are praying for the redemption of the world.

Does this expose a deep spiritual poverty within us? If we prayed this petition with a true longing that others might enter the kingdom, would our gifts for the mission of the church be so paltry, and our witness so timid? In the United States, on average only a tiny fraction of one percent of the income of Christians—about ten cents a day per person—goes toward support and partnership with churches around world. The rest of our church contributions stays in the United States, most of it for local church maintenance and usually little of that for outreach to others. We say that Jesus has given us a Great Commission to "go therefore and make disciples of all nations" (Matthew 28:19), but is ten cents a day our idea of a Great Commission? Is it not likely that our tepid giving for the Great Commission mirrors our tepid praying for the kingdom? If so, Luther's admonition to "kindle your heart to stronger and greater desires"[4] in the praying of this prayer reflects a more desperate need on our part than we may be willing to acknowledge.

To seek the reign of God places God ahead of all other claims on our affection, for to put anything else first—be it nation, family, wealth, pleasure, whatever—is to seek a kingdom that is certain to fail. One of the most popular kingdoms in North America is the pursuit of personal fulfillment through the never-ending acquisition of things or new adventures that money can buy. It is an unquenchable thirst, so Jesus asks us to give it up. The only legitimate unquenchable thirst is for God and the goodness of life with God, who the more to know is the more to desire.

> As a deer longs for flowing streams,
>   so my soul longs for you, O God.
> My soul thirsts for God,
>   for the living God (Psalm 42:1-2).

To desire God above all things may seem a bit fanatic, for we have too many examples in history, past and present, of Christians as well as people of other faiths acting arrogantly or committing atrocities in the name of God. It is easy for any of us to impose our own misguided urges on others under the illusion that we are following God. Genuine devotion to God, however, is never overbearing and abusive. It always leads to kindness.

But surely it is virtuous to put family members first, you say. Not so. To love and trust them more than God is to make of them an idol, and that is a misguided love no matter how well-intentioned. Jesus said, "Whoever loves father or mother more than me is not worthy of me; and whoever loves son or daughter more than me is not worthy of me" (Matthew 10:37). Such love is not worthy of father, mother, son, or daughter, either; for we love them best when we love Christ first, and want for them what Christ wants for them. Anything less misses the hope and vision of the kingdom.

A century ago Temple Gairdner, Anglican missionary and Arabic scholar, wrote this prayer before his marriage:

> That I may come near to her, draw me nearer to thee than to her;
> that I may know her, make me to know thee more than her; that
> I may love her with the perfect love of a perfectly whole heart,
> cause me to love thee more than her and most of all.[5]

Over and over again I have seen parents, including on occasion *this* parent, outdo themselves to give their children everything except what matters most: a life anchored in Christ. As a result our children may become clones of the culture, people who chase the dream of affluence and all the things that we are told will make us happy. But this is a self-centered life. Not surprisingly it leaves people feeling empty and unfulfilled, because they have traded their birthright for the kingdom of passing glitz.

I think of an elderly couple whose adult children never call, because the children are busy pursuing the material things that they were taught in childhood to love. The parents and their children now live prosperous but shallow lives.

I think of another family on my street, not at all prosperous. They have chosen to invest in being Christ-like parents and generous neighbors. You can sense the love and the satisfaction that has come both to the parents and children from putting God first. They are spiritual millionaires.

We are more apt to be ruined by what we love than by what we hate or fear. So getting our loves and loyalties straight is the first order of business. Jesus said that if we seek the kingdom and righteousness of God first, other things will find their proper place (see Matthew 6:33).

Longing for the Kingdom

I have noticed, especially among kids growing up in poverty, the difference that hope makes. A young person who comes to expect nothing good in life is usually headed for nothing good. But those who have seized upon a useful goal and purpose tend to rise above adverse circumstances.

Victor Frankl, the Viennese psychologist, observed the same thing as a Jewish prisoner in the Auschwitz concentration camp. He found that prisoners who survived were those who, despite the horrors they endured, could imagine a good future, while those who could not do so gave up and died. Hope was no guarantee of survival, but it saved many.

Hope makes a huge difference.

"Your life is shaped by the end you live for. You are made in the image of what you desire," Thomas Merton wrote. "To be an acorn is to have a taste for being an oak tree."[6]

In calling people to the kingdom, Jesus was offering hope, inviting us to envision the future as it will be when the reign of

God is complete. It is not just *a* hope but *the* hope, the hope that trumps all lesser hopes, the hope that empowers us to take part now in the mission of Jesus.

Jesus wants us to *long* for the kingdom. He wants us to long for it because it is *real*. It is the future already on its way. Hope in the kingdom prompts us to give our lives to others, following the example of Jesus. "If you read history," C. S. Lewis observed, "you will find that the Christians who did most for the present world were just those who thought most of the next."[7]

There are many things in life that may increase longing for the kingdom. The loss of a loved one, an illness, a disability, a broken relationship, unemployment, some grave injustice, loneliness, fear—these are among the experiences that can prompt a deep desire for the day when joy and healing will replace sorrow and pain.

Pat Brandenburg, a Bread for the World activist, endured a difficult marriage with an alcoholic husband, and she buried both of her children— Barry, who was killed at age twenty-four by a man who ran a red light, and Bradley, who died from complications of muscular dystrophy when he was forty-six. These were crushing blows. Even though Pat has health limitations, she keeps busy assisting destitute immigrants, cooking for hungry people, praying for others, and helping in a host of ways. "I don't spend much time feeling sorry for myself," she told me. "God has given me a lot of love and strength and there's too much that needs to be done." She participates already in the kingdom for which she also longs.

> As we treasure the promise of your kingdom, may it ennoble our work on earth. Our friendships, our labor, our care of the earth, our pursuit of peace, and the sharing of faith—may these all be given to you.

A longing for the kingdom is not the only possible response to setbacks, for they can also lead to self-pity, bitterness, or despair. Richard Rohr, a Franciscan priest, says, "All spirituality has to do with the question of what you do with grief and suffering and pain. If you do not, by the grace of God, transform it, you will always transmit it on to others."[8] Disappointments can turn us destructively inward rather than toward God. In that case their impact on others will also be destructive. But offered to God and transformed by God, they can lead to compassion and healing for others.

We do not need catastrophes to long for the kingdom. The love and generosity of God that we experience invite, along with gratitude, an awareness that these are only a foretaste of what God has in store for us. Eric Lidell, the British Olympic hero featured in the film, *Chariots of Fire*, won gold medals despite the fact that on religious grounds he declined to compete in a race he had been expected to win, because it was scheduled to take place on a Sunday. He said, "When I run I feel the pleasure of God." He felt the pleasure of God even more richly in Christ. That moved him to become a missionary to China, where he died after brutal treatment in a Japanese prison camp—but not before shining as an example of hope to his fellow prisoners. In the best of times and in the worst of times his heart was fixed on the kingdom.

Those of us who experience mostly the best of times also see cruelty and suffering in this world. We wait, with those who mourn, for the day when there will be no more hatred and violence, no more greed or oppression, no more pain and heartache; a day when the beauty of creation shall be complete and, rather than diminishing or destroying life, everyone will find joy in enhancing it. So we pray, "Your kingdom come, Father, and help us to long for its coming."

God's Two-fold Rule

I want to explain something so badly misunderstood that it causes many Christians to separate God's kingdom from much of life. I mention this because it greatly inhibits our prayers.

When Jesus said, "My kingdom is not from this world" (John 18:36), he did not mean "This world is of no concern to my kingdom." How could that be if Jesus has told us to pray, "Your kingdom come, your will be done *on earth* as in heaven"?

These statements of Jesus (and related biblical texts) lead us to make distinctions. One distinction is between God's saving grace, which is offered to all but received by faith; and God's providential care, which is given to everyone, scoundrels as well as saints. In both ways God exercises kingly rule that has everything to do with the world and our life in it.

> For God so loved the world that he gave his only Son, so that everyone who believes in him may not perish but may have eternal life (John 3:16). [*God's grace*]

> Your Father in heaven . . . makes his sun rise on the evil and on the good, and sends rain on the righteous and on the unrighteous (Matthew 5:45). [*God's providence*]

A related distinction is frequently made between law and gospel, with caution that we should not confuse the two. Understood in a broad sense, law includes the useful ordering of society. It's the aspect of God's providential care that lays obligations on us, as parents, citizens, employers, employees, government officials and the like, to work for the common good and the care of the earth. Doing these things somewhat well brings significant benefits to people. That fulfills part, but only part of God's purpose for us, because the law does not bestow saving, transforming grace. Even our best efforts are inadequate, so the law always judges us. The gospel, on the other hand, is God's word of forgiveness, which leads to a new life in the Spirit.

Christians of differing traditions have different ways of expressing such views. But the point I want to make is that even the most useful distinctions often get reduced to an oversimplified division of life between "spiritual" and "earthly" things. It's as though we could remove God from most of our activities and confine God to so-called spiritual matters. Aspects of life such as the workplace, dating, economic and governmental affairs, and junior high school (to name a few) get treated as off-limits to God. The result is a secular worldview. Faith is made a private matter, relegated to a small compartment of life called religion. The rest of life is lived largely without reference to God. If this is our understanding, we will neglect most of the Father's purpose for us, and so will our prayers. We may pray, "Your kingdom come," but close the door on God because the last thing we want is God messing around in nonreligious matters.

Dietrich Bonhoeffer, who was executed for his opposition to Hitler, wrote, "So long as Christ and the world are conceived as two opposing and mutually repellent spheres, man will be left to the following dilemma: he abandons reality as a whole, and places himself in one or other of the two spheres. He seeks Christ without the world, or he seeks the world without Christ."[9] So quickly do we dismantle the intent of Jesus.

God cares about us in all things of life, not merely "religious" things; and in all of life we are given opportunity to celebrate both God's grace and God's providence. So when we pray, "Your kingdom come," we ask not only that the kingdom may soon be revealed in all its glory, but also that we may in the meantime be given the wisdom and compassion to help move this troubled world closer to the intentions of God.

If we pray for the kingdom to come, we must be ready to live the way of the kingdom. It is not a prayer for staying the way we are.

6. Your Will Be Done

We are like a wayward daughter who has become a homeless drifter and is found by searching parents. They are overjoyed to find her. Of course, they have something far better in mind for her than a degenerate life on the streets. William Sloane Coffin said it well: "God loves us as we are, but much too much to leave us there."[1]

When the Father finds us, he loves us too much to leave us as we are. He wants us to be part of his kingdom. His ultimate will is to bring that kingdom to glorious completion, on earth as in heaven, and we affirm in this petition that this will happen. Meanwhile, the Father has welcomed us into the kingdom—away from our unkingdom-like captivity to sin, away from that degenerate life on the street—because he has something infinitely more wonderful in mind for us. That vision of his for us involves giving ourselves back to him in love, and giving ourselves in love to others. Because this is contrary to our wayward nature, it requires changes that are difficult and painful for us. Instead of praying, "Your will be done," we may try to press our will upon the Father, in which case the Father's response may disappoint us.

My earliest memory of disappointment in prayer came during World War II, when I was a boy and Nazi Germany invaded Norway. I followed news reports about the war with rapt attention and was alarmed by the way the Nazis were devouring country after country in Europe. It has to stop, I thought. Then I remembered words of Jesus I had memorized about the power of prayer. "Ask, and it shall be given you; seek, and ye shall find; knock, and it shall be opened unto you" (Matthew 7:7 KJV). So I prayed that the Norwegians would turn back the Nazis. I prayed it again and again, confidently expecting that the Nazis would experience a stunning defeat. Not only were the Nazis doing evil, but the Norwegians were 98 percent Lutheran! Surely, the prayer had to be a dead ringer for the will of God. But to my dismay, the German forces (many of them Lutheran) swept through Norway and occupied the country.

That experience raised for me the problem of evil as well as the problem of unanswered prayer. I began to realize that both were more complicated than I had been led to believe. Was my prayer not a good one? I think it was, except for my failure to submit the matter to God's will, which seemed to me beyond doubt. I am still far from understanding this well, but I am content to believe that the prayer helped in some way. It certainly helped me learn that there is more than a little mystery to life and that God's ways are beyond my own. It also helped me realize that even the seemingly most obvious solution must be entrusted to God. After all, in his time of greatest agony Jesus prayed, "*Abba*, Father, for you all things are possible; remove this cup from me; yet, not what I want, but what you want" (Mark 14:36). Jesus not only taught "your will be done." He lived it.

Countless times since that boyhood prayer I have begged, bargained, and arm-twisted to get God to see things my way. I have asked God to rubber-stamp my wishes and bless them. It is a type of praying that we relinquish with utmost reluctance, because we are afraid of the path that God may have us take.

Even when we know how essential it is to reflect patiently on what God may want for us, we find ways of holding back. I am amazed at how quickly after praying "Your will be done" I can revert to seeking my own, so instinctively captive is our will. It is this captive will of ours that Jesus carried to the cross in order to break its power over us. But even with its power broken, if we pray for God's will and then follow our own, we are imposing our intentions on God. All the while God has much better plans for us than we have for ourselves.

I have criticized begging prayers. However, there is a sense in which begging prayers are exactly what our prayers should be. What is God's will, but that we come as little children to our dear *Abba*, totally dependent upon him, putting our complete trust in him, and pouring out to him every feeling, every need. God is not put off by such honesty—the Psalms are filled with it and God cherishes it as an expression of love. But unless it is then entrusted to God, we make God an object of our manipulation. The kind of begging the Father wants most of all is empty hands and hearts that need to be filled with the grace of forgiveness and the desire to do God's will. The Father's will for us is not, in the first instance, a morally upright life, but a contrite heart. If moral rectitude leads to pride and self-righteousness, it ruins our relationship with God. "My son, my daughter, give me your heart," the Father says. The response that flows from this request delights the Lord, for it is the response of love.

Acceptance and Action
Response there will be. For to pray, "Your will be done," is not simply passive trust in God, a kind of fatalistic acceptance of

letting happen to us whatever is beyond our control—though such acceptance can also be a form of trust. For the most part, however, the petition is a prayer that we may actively follow the way of the kingdom. As Paul Scherer said, putting our life in God's hands "is not at all where we quit; it is where we may truly begin."[2] We are not powerless. God's way of answering many of our prayers is to give us the strength and wisdom to do what we need to do. We dare not give thanks for God's creation and proceed to despoil it. We cannot pray for employment but not go job hunting, pray for good government but not bother to vote, pray for good grades but not study, pray for hungry people but ignore opportunities to help them, or pray that people come to know Christ but keep our faith hidden.

> *Your will be done, Father.*
> *What a magnificent exchange:*
> *your wisdom for our foolishness,*
> *your steadfast love for our*
> *waywardness.*

Robin Sonnenberg desired God's will when she prayed with her son from his infancy: "Lord, help our dear Jacob someday marry a Christian wife, and may our families love each other." Her husband Roger says, "Each time the prayer is spoken, Robin believes God is listening and preparing such a wife for Jacob." And Jacob has grown up to believe it too. On occasions when Robin would omit the petition, Jacob would say, "Mom, you forgot that other part." Now a seventeen-year-old teenager, Jacob approaches friendships and dating with a sense of Christian maturity, and although they no longer have bedtime prayers together, Jacob knows that his mother continues to offer that prayer each day.[3]

Both acceptance and action are required of us. We shape life by choices we make, but life also shapes us—sometimes handing us unexpected and undeserved opportunities, and at other times setbacks. It raises some people from obscurity and foils the ambitions of others. To one is given prosperity and acclaim, to another struggle for survival. Surprise is common, as most of us have discovered, because life as it unfolds is full of twists and turns that we cannot anticipate. The experiences of marriage, children, and career, for example, may be at once more difficult and more satisfying than expected. But whatever our situation, whether urchin or king, it provides the raw material out of which we are challenged to become a more finished product for God. Our life on earth is preparation for eternity.

A prisoner, Jon Marc Taylor, whom I am assisting a bit with an appeal for clemency, has been reading a book by Archbishop Desmond Tutu of South Africa. In it Tutu describes the long and seemingly hopeless struggle against apartheid and speaks of prayers offered in the face of repression as "a kind of theological whistling in the dark."[4] It is an appropriate parallel to his own situation, considering the long odds against clemency, which Taylor both deserves and deeply craves. But it is also a reminder that God has plans for each of us that may or may not coincide with our own. The apostle Paul would add that "in all things"—no matter how awful the circumstance—"God works for the good of those who love him" (Romans 8:28 NIV). This I believe, though it is more than I can fathom.

Discerning God's Will

Because it looks forward to the completion of God's will in the kingdom, "Your will be done" becomes also a listening prayer, a prayer that we may discern the purpose that God has for us in the kingdom now. So we tell God of our desires and release control of them. We ask God to replace our foolishness with his wisdom. Then we need to listen. Listening to God and reflecting on God's will not only informs the thoughts we offer to God, but more importantly it opens us to receive what God desires to give.

But how do we perceive the will of God? How can we know what God wants us to do? Although we seldom have complete clarity in specific situations, we do have guidance from (1) the Bible and its witness to the purpose of God for us in Christ. Our prayers, informed by that written word, can open our minds to the will of God. We can also get help from (2) sisters and brothers in Christ, or family members and friends whose judgment we have reason to trust, and saints through the ages who have left their example. (3) The hymns and prayers of the church are a rich source of wisdom. In addition God has given us (4) special talents and interests that can help us decide, for example, what kind of career or voluntary activities to pursue. (5) Above all, we are told to make Christ-like love our aim.

Part of God's will is that we struggle to seek God's will. That struggle strengthens our faith by forcing us to exercise it. This way it acts like roots growing stronger as a tree resists the wind.

My father used to tell me, "Whatever you decide to do in life, whether you are a missionary or a bus driver, the main thing is that you do it for God." That didn't seem to me as a boy to be of much help in thinking about a career, but it probably was the best advice I ever got. And my father, by his example, gave me a model that brought the gospel of Jesus to life. A few years ago I was sorting old photographs when I ran across one of myself at age eight or nine. It showed a scrawny boy with little round glasses and rumpled shirt and hair—about the most unimpressive kid you could imagine. But in large letters my father had printed across the bottom, "A boy, a man of God." It immediately became one of my favorites. With such help we learn to seek the will of God.

While growing up, I always had some idea of what I wanted to do in life. The idea would change from time to time when I found something more attractive to turn to. It was like crossing a stream by stepping on rocks that rise above the water. You leave one rock only when you have another one to land on. Then one summer after my first year of college I found myself uncertain about what I wanted to do. I had never felt such uncertainty before. It left me standing in midstream with no next rock to keep me out of the water. I had jumped from psychology to law to journalism, but now none of them seemed right. So I prayed. And I talked with my brother Paul, who had launched a promising career as a weekly newspaper editor. I never heard a voice from heaven or felt a tap on the shoulder, but as the weeks went by there gradually grew in my mind the sense that just as Paul felt called to serve God in public life as a layman, God was calling me to the pastoral ministry. So that's what I did, and I have never regretted it.

Not every vocational decision is made so easily. For many, careers change a few times. Writer Frederich Buechner somewhere suggested, "Combine what you enjoy doing with what the world needs." That's good advice, and it can be part of the way in which one discerns God's will. Many times on various matters, however, we are required to make decisions despite uncertainty, and all we can do is use our best judgment, with prayer, and offer the outcome to God. Sometimes that means living with the consequences, even if hindsight may reveal a foolish decision. Sometimes it means struggling to unearth God's will in matters about which Christians sharply differ. But these can become opportunities for us to grow in faith and forgiveness.

Praying in Jesus's Name
When Jesus urged us to pray, he promised that we *will* receive. He did not, however, promise that we would get exactly what we asked for, any more than a good parent would give children

anything they wanted—a sure way to ruin them. True, the Gospel of John contains a clear promise from Jesus that the Father will give us whatever we ask; but he attached a special condition: "If you ask anything of the Father *in my name*, he will give it to you" (John 16:23).

What does it mean to pray in the name of Jesus? It cannot mean requesting anything under the sun and adding the words, "in Jesus's name." I did that when I prayed for the Norwegians and it didn't work, at least not the way I intended. Conversely, the Lord's Prayer itself makes no mention of the name of Jesus. To pray in Jesus's name means to pray with faith in Jesus as the way to the Father, and with the desire to follow him faithfully. The heart of such prayer is, "Your kingdom come, your will be done," for that is what Jesus desires, and what we through Jesus also desire most.

Luke's version of the Lord's Prayer omits "Your will be done." Perhaps it was the more original version or perhaps the gospel writer decided to skip a line that was expressed well enough by "Your kingdom come." But in the words of Jesus that follow, we are given an explanation that sheds light on the entire prayer and these petitions in particular. Jesus emphasized how much the Father wants us to come to him and ask for what we need. Ask and you will receive, he urged. If your children ask you for a fish or an egg, Jesus said, would you give them a snake or a scorpion? He added, "If you then, who are evil, know how to give good gifts to your children, how much more will the heavenly Father give *the Holy Spirit* to those who ask him" (Luke 11:13). That is a clear indication of what we are to be praying for—not wealth or personal advantages, but the Holy Spirit who brings us to faith and makes us alive in Christ, and who, we are told, is the down payment of our inheritance in the kingdom (Ephesians 1:14). To ask for the Holy Spirit, then, is to ask for help in planting our hopes more fully in God. It is to pray for God's kingdom to come and God's will to be done in us—another way of praying in the name of Jesus.

When Jesus urged us to pray in his name, he added, "Ask and you will receive, so that your joy may be complete" (John 16:24). That tells us something truly important. To seek God's will is not the gritting of teeth. It is the pursuit of true joy, one of the gifts of the Spirit. So we give praise for the opportunities and successes we may have, and for the pleasures of family and friendship that God gives, along with the setbacks and hard knocks of life. All are to be received with thanksgiving, seen as occasions for growth, and offered to God with the prayer that God's will may be done.

> *Dear Father, take our sins and successes, our hopes and fears. Discard what is worthless and refashion what is good.*

On Earth As in Heaven

"Your will be done *on earth as it is in heaven*." It could not be any clearer. Precisely *because* we fix our hope in the coming kingdom, we are to desire that God's will be done on this earth. We do not pray that God's will be done in heaven, for it is already being done there. But we are forbidden to say, "The world is going to hell and God's will doesn't have a chance here. Doing God's will on earth is a waste of time and of no consequence. All that matters is the saving of souls for heaven." Such a stance is a refusal to love the world that God loves and a rejection of this petition.

"Not everyone who says to me, 'Lord, Lord,' will enter the kingdom of heaven," Jesus said, "but only the one who does the will of my Father in heaven" (Matthew 7:21). That we never do the Father's will anywhere near to perfection on this earth is no excuse for not trying, for we will never honor God's holy name perfectly either, or strive for God's kingdom perfectly, or forgive others perfectly, or trust God perfectly to take care of us. We pray that God's will be done on earth *because* we do it so poorly and need help to do it better. That we do so is God's great desire, so it must become our great desire as well.

This world is not our lasting home, but it is still the handiwork of God, a world of stunning beauty, full of living things and precious resources that God created. And God has asked us to take care of it for future generations. It is a world that God sent his only Son to save; and it is the place where we are to love and serve God with all our heart. Though we are saved by grace through faith, our work on earth is connected to our life in the resurrection. What we do on earth is related to God's eternal purpose for us in Christ. Why else would Jesus teach that faithfulness now in small things will be richly rewarded in heaven, and urge us to store up treasures there?

> *"Your will be done" is no small prayer, for it touches on the mystery of life, the mystery of evil, and the mystery of God.*
> *And yet they are mysteries revealed sufficiently for us to know that God cares deeply, suffers with us and for us, and has set out on a plan to unite all things to himself in Christ.*

Relinquishment

I still do not know why God allowed the Nazis to occupy Norway, or why the Nazi regime was allowed to ravage nations and crush the lives and hopes of countless millions. I don't believe that was God's will, except in some permissive sense. Jesus came into this world to overcome evil and to take our sin upon himself. This is how relentlessly determined God is to destroy evil. I think of this when I see the tyranny and brutality that is inflicted on nations and individuals today, a glance into the bowels of hell. Pain and cruelty, like death, are not good. They reflect our fallen condition. It is we humans, however, not God, who are called to account for what we do or fail to do.

I recall a "Pontius Puddle" cartoon strip that showed two people. The first one said, "Sometimes I am tempted to ask God why he allows so many people to go hungry." The second asks him, "Why don't you?" And the first replies, "Because I'm afraid he might ask me the same question."

Though permitting evil for a time, God can use the evil that befalls us to accomplish good. As a youth, Joseph was torn by his brothers from his father, family and homeland, and sold as a slave in Egypt, where he was imprisoned on false charges. Years later, after he had risen to power, he revealed himself to his shaken brothers, saying, "Even though you intended to do harm to me, God intended it for good" (Genesis 50:20). Centuries later the apostle Paul expressed joy for being imprisoned because it served to advance the Gospel (Philippians 1:12-26). He believed that his considerable suffering was being used by God to accomplish good, and therefore was an occasion for joy.

"Your will be done" turns us to God where we find our true freedom and our true self. Just as we need to die each day to sin and rise with Christ to a new life, so also we need to submit the desires of our heart to God, some of which we know to be wrong, and others we may think to be right. All of them are to be given to God. Then God can return and honor those that are good and transform or discard those that are not, close doors that we would open, and open doors to us of which we are unaware. We discover that we pray for ourselves when we pray against ourselves by surrendering our will to God. If God does not want something for us, how can it be good? And if God desires something for us, how can it be bad?

JoAnne Lyon tells of her resentment toward God because of her inability for many years to bear children. Confessing this, she saw two choices:

> I could either *relinquish* my infertility or *resign* myself to it. The difference between the two is subtle but powerful. I picture it this way: to relinquish a circumstance is to approach God with an open hand, saying, "Here it is, Lord. I don't know what to do with this, but I look forward to what you will do." Relinquishment is not an attempt to second-guess God or to manipulate him. It is an act of willing surrender. To resign, on the other hand, is to approach God with a closed hand—a fist—saying, "If this is the way life has to be, then I'll grit my teeth and bear it. I'll accept this thing, but nothing on earth will ever make me like it." Resignation accepts the circumstance but stubbornly resists God in the process.[5]

Relinquishment, she says, changes the focus "from the good thing that God might provide . . . to God himself." That is a key insight. We were made for communion with God, and without God there is no contentment. But it is God, not contentment, that we seek in this petition.

"Your will be done" is no small prayer, for it touches on the mystery of life, the mystery of evil, and the mystery of God. And yet they are mysteries revealed sufficiently for us to know that God cares deeply, suffers with us and for us, and has set out on a plan to unite all things to

> If God does not want something for us, how can it be good? And if God desires something for us, how can it be bad?

himself in Christ. That points us to the promised kingdom and the time when God brings the whole plan of salvation to completion. All wrongs will be righted, and we ourselves will be changed to fully reflect the heart of God.

Until then we invite God to shape our life and the lives of others, for we are a work in progress.

7. Give Us Daily Bread—I

The prayer of Jesus anchors us in God. First we approach God as our Father. Then we pray, "May *your* holy name be honored, *your* kingdom come, *your* will be done." In this way we acknowledge that God alone is the foundation and center of our lives.

Now, however, the prayer shifts. We ask the Father to take care of *us*. "Give *us* each day *our* daily bread." It is a simple petition with profound implications.

Although the petition, along with those that follow, moves us in a different direction, it is intimately tied to the previous petitions. Just as the whole prayer is a prayer for the kingdom and therefore an affirmation of hope, this petition also affirms that hope. It does so, first of all, because only as we trust God to take care of us can we quit worrying and become free to pursue our life in the kingdom.

I find that I must relearn this every day.

Bread and Hope

Trust sets us free. Trusting God for daily bread releases us to honor God's name, seek God's will, and put God's kingdom first. Conversely, putting our hope in the kingdom gives us confidence that our earthly needs will be taken care of. In this way the prayer for daily bread is a prayer of hope.

But there is another way in which the petition expresses hope. The prophets sometimes pictured the reign of God as God coming to feed his people. For people to whom hunger was a frequent guest, it must have had an especially strong appeal. "On this mountain the LORD of hosts will make for all peoples a feast of rich food, a feast of well-aged wines. . . . And . . . he will swallow up death forever" (Isaiah 25:6-7). The petition for daily bread focuses on this aspect of the kingdom.

Jesus's multiplication of the loaves gave what the prayer promised. His feeding of a large crowd was recorded not four, but six times in the gospels—the only miracle given such prominence. It signaled that Jesus was the Messiah, because it re-enacted the time when Israel was in the wilderness and received *manna* from heaven, and it brought to mind the prophecies about God spreading a feast for all people. The earliest Christians believed that both the feeding and the Lord's Supper proclaimed hope in the kingdom, because both pointed to the time when we will celebrate the feast with Christ in heaven. The Lord's Prayer was included in the communion liturgy at least partly because it also reflects this expectation.

Which leads me to say—because it has helped me pray this petition—that we cannot be certain about the exact meaning of the Greek word usually translated *daily* (in "daily bread"). Scholars have come up with several other interpretations; but the leading alternative and preference of many (footnoted in some translations), is *tomorrow*. In that case the petition would read, "Give us today our bread for tomorrow." Some who favor *bread for tomorrow* (or bread

> *"Grace our table with your presence, and give us a foretaste of the feast to come."*
>
> Lutheran Book of Worship, p. 86

to come) believe it refers to the bread that Jesus said we would break with him in the messianic feast in heaven. In this petition, then, we would be asking for that heavenly bread today—the bread of life that we receive in Holy Communion.[1] This interpretation further emphasizes the way in which the prayer of Jesus keeps focusing on our ultimate hope.

I find this interpretation attractive and plausible, though far from certain. For my own reflection I have come to accept that the petition refers both to daily bread and the bread of life. Each way, for very different reasons, it celebrates hope. It reminds me as well that because of that hope we should enjoy every meal in the presence of Christ, just as the rest of everyday life is to be hallowed by his presence.

All That We Need

The prayer for daily bread is modest. It asks for enough. Not wants, but needs. Not too little, not too much. It is a prayer for contentment. Jesus warned people not to covet riches or worry about food and clothing. He knew that poor people were especially tempted to let worry grind them down; but he was far tougher on the affluent. "It is easier for a camel to go through the eye of a needle than for someone who is rich to enter the kingdom of God" (Luke 18:25), he told his astonished disciples. "Sell your possessions and give to the poor," he urged (Luke 12:33 NIV). Most of us who enjoy prosperity pay scant attention to these words of Jesus because they threaten our zone of comfort.

Praying for what we need does not mean that God allows only the barest necessities, because beauty, pleasure, laughter, and love are priceless gifts of God. God takes delight in our delight. We can spread the table well on occasion and give glory to God in doing so. Jesus's attendance at a wedding feast and his dining and drinking with social outcasts—signs of the kingdom—tell us something of this.

Still, it is not easy for us to know where to draw the line between acceptable wants and excess; so this petition invites careful reflection and a willingness to listen to God about matters that deeply affect us and others. If enjoying abundance is part of the kingdom, so are generosity and shouldering the cross. Both feasting and fasting have their place. "It is sometimes necessary to deny yourselves some of the good and beautiful things of this life in order to prepare the heart for the best that God wants to give—or in order to communicate His love and joy to others about you," wrote Leslie Brandt.[2]

God gives us the responsibility of using faithfully what has been entrusted to us, and there lies the freedom either to abuse God's gifts or to give ourselves more fully to Jesus. Precise instructions on what to spend or not spend is not God's way. God wants our hearts and has left us guidance enough. The problem for most of us is not that we can't understand what Jesus has asked of us. Our problem is a shortage of love to act on the understanding we have.

Daily bread—all that we need for body and life—sounds simple enough; but for most of us it entails complexities that often lie beyond our understanding or control. These prompt us to cry out for help. Give us wisdom and strength to deal with the difficulties of life, we pray.

A friend of mine who married in his early forties brought his bride into their new home, where they spent their first night mopping, cleaning, and fixing the plumbing on a toilet that suddenly overflowed. It was a honeymoon fit for the real world. That kind of experience enriches the meaning of this petition, for under such circumstances to believe that God gives us what we need requires trust and humility, not to mention a sense of humor. But the prayer is also in order when a workload overwhelms, a car breaks down, a job is lost, or sickness or an accident occurs. None of these is to be left passively to God without a response of our own. Rather our action and that of others can be turned over to God. We need to entrust ourselves to God always, but at such times we are made more keenly aware of our limitations.

Life is uneven. To the disparities of health, intelligence, ability, and personality we add our own sins and shortcomings. Yet we are to believe that God has given us what we need to fulfill his intentions for us, and that God can use even our weaknesses to do so. "Out of the ashes of our failures He brings forth meaning and purpose."[3]

The petition offers us assurance that God will help us deal with limitations. Couples, for example, discover that they bring into a marriage their respective flaws. Compatibility is never perfect, so compromise and forgiveness are essential. These factors multiply when children come along. Parents may feel driven to pray, "Why, Lord, did you not give me a better spouse and more compliant children?" But God uses marriage and the family as a school for growth, for learning how to get along, how to make a go of it under sometimes trying circumstances, how to forgive and be forgiven. So "Give us this day our daily bread"—all that we need—is the right prayer. In fact, part of the answer to the prayer is the problem that prompts it, because one of our biggest needs is coming to terms with our own limitations.

Another need is learning to love and serve those with whom God has placed us. For this, God provides social structures, such as the family and the workplace, to help insure that we do our part in obtaining daily bread for ourselves and others. By working, for example, we help support and care for our loved ones, and serve the needs of others who support and care for theirs. Unbelievers, as well as believers, do this, often serving God and sometimes neighbor unaware. But when our work is intentionally offered to God, it is enriched by faith. The doing of good is enriched as well.

Coveting

Responsibility of this kind is not always easy to accept. Inundated with attractions that whet our appetites and raise our expectations, we may begin to view our own humdrum life with discontent. Discontent can be good if it leads to constructive change. Frequently, however, it prompts us to desire what is not rightfully ours and what is not good for us. Coveting is the opposite of asking for daily bread. It is the enemy of happiness because it enlarges our appetite for what we do not have rather than enlarging our gratitude.

Let me illustrate with two of the most deadly forms of coveting.

The first is greed. This is a particularly tough problem for those of us who live in industrialized nations, because ours is a prosperous, consumer-driven culture. We are constantly shown new things to get or do with our money. Our values, and therefore our lives, are extensively shaped by the notion that we are what we have. We are led to believe that happiness lies in the next purchase or the next vacation. The problem is not that the things we buy are all bad, for many of them contribute to our well being and create employment for others. The problem is that the affluent life can capture our hearts and *become* our life. The purpose of God for us is forgotten. "Give us what we need" becomes "Satisfy our growing appetite for things." Greed has been called "the unchallenged sin in the American church."[4] But the pursuit of fleeting advantages leaves our hearts empty, and that is why the life Jesus offers us is immeasurably better.[5]

Lust is another form of coveting. Greed and lust are closely related, because the celebration of casual sex has become a high dollar preoccupation of the media and the public. "One of the worst effects of coveting is that it spoils relationships," observes Marva Dawn in *Unfettered Hope*.[6] That is true of coveting possessions, but at least as true about coveting sex. When we lust, our glands control us, and we want to use others for our own gratification. Lust may take the form of infatuation, which often masquerades as falling in love. Infatuation is a kind of intoxication, but we do not think clearly while "under the influence." Relating to someone in this way does not lay a foundation for a deep and enduring relationship. It does not prepare us for commitment or for the ordinariness of life. By seizing the illusion of intimacy in order to escape loneliness, lust actually invests in loneliness.

Lust is the opposite of *agape*, love that seeks the good of another through the love of Christ. In genuine love we give ourselves to the well being of another. Non-Christians do this too. But people who have been moved by the self-giving love of God see the well being of others through the heart and mind of Christ. That is the deepest of loves.

Just as people sometimes talk—quite mistakenly, I believe—about victimless crimes, it is easy to think of coveting as a victimless sin. After all, coveting is only a private thought in the mind, and what harm can that do? Plenty. First, private thoughts lead to action. Jesus said that "out of the heart come evil intentions, murder, adultery, fornication, theft, false witness, slander" (Matthew 15:19). He might have added spoiled relationships. Second, as Dietrich Bonhoeffer said, "When you have made the eye the instrument of impurity, you cannot see God with it."[7] Neither the eye nor the heart can be given to God when filled with illicit desire. The desire that closes the heart to God also closes the heart to one's neighbor. Preoccupied with gratifying itself, the heart is distracted from the needs of others, including the real needs of the person to whom our desire may have drawn us.

This petition is inviting us to take a better path. Greed indicates a wrong relationship to possessions, just as lust indicates a wrong relationship to sexual desire. Possessions and sexual desire, far from being intrinsically wrong, come from God. Not money, but the *love* of money is the root of much evil. Not sexual desire, but *misplaced* sexual desire is sinful.

Behind the sin in each case is a wonderful part of God's creation. Received with thanksgiving and honored by using them as God intended, possessions and sexual desire are magnificent gifts. The petition affirms this by suggesting the right way to relate to God and our earthly needs. We are to entrust them to God.

Trust

The father of a devout church-going family that I once knew had immigrated from Europe as a youth and had achieved some success as a butcher. Over the years he had invested his savings in the stock market. When the stock market took a steep dive, he became so distraught that he killed his wife and himself. That is an extreme example of

> *Father, give us courage to trust you for every need, that we may live as children of the kingdom.*

misplaced trust. But any one of us could serve as a more ordinary example. We worry. We spend our lives accumulating assets that cannot last. We desire what God does not see fit to give.

When Jesus asks us to trust God for daily bread, he is telling us to surrender a powerful natural impulse. He is asking us to quit worrying about tomorrow—not meaning don't fix the leaking roof or call a doctor when you need one, but do what you can each day and leave the worrying to God. Worry is the opposite of trust. It is also the opposite of prayer, because you can take worry and transform it instantly into prayer by simply offering it up to God.

Most of those whom Jesus told not to worry struggled daily for survival. Theirs was a hand-to-mouth existence, as it is for much of the world's population today. That did not, for them or for us, preclude planning, but it did underscore that God has set limits on our ability to know what lies ahead—and that is surely a kindness. So we are asked to receive each day what we need and stop worrying about things we cannot know or control. "Today's trouble is enough for today," said Jesus (Matthew 6:34).

We worry and covet because we instinctively seek familiar forms of security. We are like the grandmother of Eddie Ricken-backer, famous test pilot when airplanes were in their infancy. Upon learning what he was going to do, she advised him always to fly slow and close to the ground. That is a picture of our own spiritual timidity. It is only by entrusting our earthly security to God and taking wings of faith that we can soar. But we will do that only if we are captivated by a better vision: the promise of the kingdom that is ours in Christ. So intimately are trust and hope related.

Adversity
To pray for daily bread is to trust God also in adversity. Among those for whom I am currently praying are three couples, each with a spouse facing life-threatening cancer, and in one instance the medical certainty of a slow, painful death. Two of the three couples have small children. The third is Dave Becker,[8] a friend from my youth who was nearly killed in the Korean war and, after much painful surgery, had only partial vision and mobility. Yet he never lost his faith or his winsome disposition. Now he faces terminal cancer—challenging enough. In addition, his four-year-old

grandson, Andrew, just lost a long and agonizing struggle of his own with cancer. Dave at seventy-two? One can understand that. But Andrew at four?

And what about holocaust victims? Or other innocent millions who are killed, raped, tortured, abused? They may be asking, "Why, Lord?" But if we are among the comparatively privileged, we should be asking that too. "Why, Lord, should I have had so many advantages in life and such good health?" It is one thing for me to trust God with all that I need, but what about Dave, or Andrew's parents? What about children who have been abandoned, maimed, or brutalized? People who are ridiculed, terrified, or in pain? Those for whom hunger is a way of life and early death? When I think what it takes for them to believe that God is providing all that they need, I am humbled—by Andrew, for one. When his little body had taken all the punishment it could stand, his mother, holding him on her lap, said, "It's all right, Andrew, you can let go. Jesus is here to take you by the hand." Andrew reached out and said, "Jesus, Jesus," and breathed his last.

When Jesus told his followers not to be afraid, he knew they would face hardship, persecution, and, in some cases, death as a consequence of their faith. It was important for them to trust that God would give them all that they needed, no matter how difficult the circumstances.

Of course, if this short life is all that we live for, such risks are unacceptable. Setbacks then threaten the little that we have. The promise of an eternal kingdom, however, allows us to see things from a very different perspective. Much that does not compute in this life will be amply rewarded in the resurrection.

The opposite of fear is faith. Trust in God overcomes our fear and gives us courage for faithful living. We may need courage not to withhold our talent but offer it fully in service to God. We may need courage to overcome peer pressure, courage to turn a lack of marital prospects from a source of self-pity into a vocational calling, courage to risk the ridicule of others by letting our faith be known and speaking the truth in love, courage to sell possessions and give to the poor. Or we may need courage to face persecution and death for Jesus. But we cannot have such courage without trusting that God will take care of every need. Trust gives strength for obedience.

When I was a little boy I had a terrible earache, so my mother took me to the doctor. I was afraid of what the doctor might do, and my fears soon turned into panic. He pulled out an alarmingly long needle—clearly an instrument of torture in the hands of a ruthless man. I screamed in terror. But my mother and a nurse held me still, while the doctor lanced a boil in my ear. There was a burst of awful pain—then sweet relief. The pain was gone. The doctor smiled and gave me a lollipop. My reaction had been a typical human reaction to adversity. Like that physician, however, God has only our healing in mind, but knows that sometimes we must be wounded before we can heal. And maybe the wounding prepares us to bring healing to others.

"I have never heard anyone say the really deep lessons of life have come in times of ease and comfort. But, I have heard many saints say every significant advance ever made in entering into the depth of God's love and growing deep with [God], have come through suffering," John Piper has written.[9]

Joni Eareckson Tada lost the use of both legs and arms in a diving accident when she was seventeen years old. Despite that loss of mobility, she has achieved fame as an accomplished artist. She paints by holding the brush between her teeth. Instead of becoming embittered, she gave her ability and disability to God and sees her accident as part of God's plan for her, "the harder yet richer path." She has touched thousands of lives with her witness to Christ and assists the disabled in dozens of countries. Thirty-six years after her accident she visited the pool of Bethesda in Old Jerusalem, where Jesus had healed a man who had been paralyzed for thirty-eight years. As much as she longed for her own physical healing there, she acknowledged to God the more important healing of her soul. "I know I wouldn't know you. . . . I wouldn't love and trust you . . . were it not for this wheelchair."[10]

The Apostle Paul stands out as a giant in seeing purpose in suffering. Beaten bloody with rods, exhausted, imprisoned, and shackled in Philippi (Acts 16), he and Silas prayed and sang hymns in the middle of the night, as the other prisoners listened. Later, a prisoner elsewhere, he could write a letter of joy to the Christians of Philippi, thanking God that his latest imprisonment had served to advance the cause of the gospel. In writing to the Corinthian Christians, Paul told of the hard knocks he had taken: whippings, beatings, stonings, hunger, shipwreck—and a great personal burden, his mysterious "thorn in the flesh." Three times Paul begged God to remove it, but God said to him, perhaps through a long and dark silence, "My grace is sufficient for you, for power is made perfect in weakness" (2 Corinthians 12:9). So Paul celebrated his weakness.

Because of the kingdom, already here in Christ but still to come in its fullness, we can pray for daily bread trusting that even when "all that we need" seems denied us, even when life falls apart, our body breaks down, and memory slips away, God provides. So we pray for the gift of trust, knowing that any present hardship is transformed into preparation for that completeness of life beyond the grave.

> And when this cup you give is filled to brimming
>   with bitter suffering, hard to understand,
> We take it thankfully and without trembling
>   out of so good and so beloved a hand.[11]

Dietrich Bonhoeffer, a leader of the underground church in Germany during the Nazi regime, wrote the above lines while awaiting his execution. Luther's hymn, "A Mighty Fortress is Our God," conveyed similar thoughts centuries earlier:

> Were they to take our house, goods, honor, child, or spouse,
> Though life be wrenched away, they cannot win the day.
> The kingdom's ours forever![12]

As the Psalm on which that hymn was based says, "God is our refuge and strength, a very present help in trouble" (Psalm 46:1). It does not say God is an escape from trouble. Trust is essential.

8. Give Us Daily Bread—II

Each day is a gift from God, a wonder to cherish. Out of love God provides us with daily bread—all that we need. To believe that God really does this, and to trust God for it, should fill us with gratitude so immense that we overflow with praise and thanksgiving. The result is the further gift of contentment, for just as coveting destroys contentment, gratitude ushers it in.

Thanks and Praise

It is ironic that those who seem most thankful are often people in precarious health or people who have gone through a life-threatening experience. But perhaps that is not surprising. When we are young and strong we tend to take our days and our health for granted, but doing so is a great personal loss. I am no exception.

One of the best things that ever happened to me was an accident in Africa from which I narrowly escaped death. I was traveling for Christian Children's Fund from Kampala, Uganda's capital, to the Rakai district where the HIV-AIDS virus was first discovered, in order to visit some devastated communities and observe an innovative AIDS program sponsored by World Vision. Seven of us were sitting on two wooden benches that flanked either side of the van behind the driver's seat. The driver got us off to a late start because his four-year-old daughter had come down with malaria, so he drove at high speed in order to regain lost time.

Shortly after crossing the equator, we encountered a heavy downpour. Sensing that he was going too fast, the driver put his foot on the brake pedal. The van, with its treadless tires, instantly skidded across the highway out of control. It hit a ditch, flipped over several times, and landed upside down, badly crushed. Miraculously all of us crawled out hurt but alive. I spent that first sleepless night with a back and leg injury. Never have I been in such pain, nor ever so grateful to be alive. Tears and laughter flowed together. With the light of dawn an ancient morning prayer of the church kept running through my mind: "Almighty and everlasting God, who has safely brought us to the beginning of this day [Thank you, Lord!], defend us in the same with your mighty power, and grant that this day we fall into no sin, neither run into any kind of danger [Yes!]. . . ."

Most of us are tepid thankers and praisers. Our private prayers probably reflect this, and in my experience so do our prayers in church, where we spend more time and get more specific about those in trouble than we do about reasons for praising God. Each morning when I go jogging I am astounded by the beauty of God's creation and the miracle of life, my own included. I marvel that this reality does not instill in me a constant sense of praise. But my attention span is short and gratitude quickly slips away. Should we let the birds outdo us in giving praise? If heaven and nature burst into song at the coming of the earth's king, is there any reason why we who have been redeemed should not also excel at this?

There are reasons, of course. One is that we get so busy God is easily forgotten. Another is that we take God largely for granted, and from little appreciation comes little praise. Yet another is that we tend to think that what we have is the result of our own hard work, mistaking the source of our daily bread; and so we applaud ourselves rather than God.

Strangely, those with the least are often the most grateful. I ran into an amazing example of this in Mozambique during a time of civil war and severe drought. A few of us came upon an encampment of several dozen people who had fled their village in search of food. Many villagers had already died, and these survivors were living in makeshift tents, foraging for berries and nuts and little creatures that supplemented their meager ration of daily grain from CARE. They had virtually nothing but the tattered clothes they wore and a few pots for cooking. But they were alive. We spent some time listening to wrenching personal stories. As we got ready to leave, some of the women began to sing and clap and dance in a circle, their faces beaming as they moved first in one direction, then the other. They repeated the same words over and over. I finally asked someone, "What are they singing?" The man translated, "We have food. We have clothes. We have everything!" These people, destitute beyond belief, were rich in gratitude.[1]

Bread for Others

The simple petition for daily bread casts a wider net than meets the eye. It is a prayer for enough, the placing of trust in God for all of our earthly needs. This sets us free to seek first the kingdom of God. For all of this we lift our hearts in praise and thanksgiving to the Father.

> "Lord, give bread to the hungry, and hunger of you to those who have bread."

But the petition sends another essential message to us. Because it is not *my* bread but *our* bread for which we pray, we ask that others too may receive what they need. This points us toward the common good and away from lonely acquisition. What we wish for ourselves—daily bread and the bread of life—we also wish for others. We ask God to help us give as we have been given, just as we seek to forgive as we have been forgiven.

How quickly we forget the hardship of others when we live in relative ease. Not long ago I received a letter about a previous book of mine from Mary Murphy, who teaches math at Smith College. She wrote:

> Four years ago I spent a month living with six Catholic missionaries in the outskirts of Santo Domingo. We washed clothes and bedding by hand; we spent hours collecting and purifying water whenever it chose to trickle through the spigots; we traveled on unbelievably crowded, noisy buses to go anywhere. When I got home, I stood at the kitchen sink marveling in gratitude for the potable water that flowed from the tap. I gave thanks for my washing machine and my car. And then, well, I began to forget how privileged I am. My friends in Los Alcarrizos are still straining their water through rags and boiling large kettles of it for twenty minutes on a tiny, barely adequate, stove, but I've gone back to turning on the tap without a thought.[2]

As her letter implies, thanks for daily bread is more than a nod to God before we stuff ourselves. It does not mean thanking God that we are not like others—poor, hungry, homeless, or even as that welfare recipient. That would mimic the smugness of the Pharisee who thanked God that he was better than others (Luke 18:1-14)—altered slightly to thank God that we are better *off* than others. Far from saluting God for our prosperity, genuine thanksgiving generates a deep desire that others may also have enough to meet their needs. If praying for daily bread means to pray for enough, then surely the implication is that when we have more than enough we will share the "more" so that others may also have enough. Such sharing is an indication that our hope in Christ is deep and true.

James Mulholland was watching a Christian from Sudan being interviewed on television. "How can our rich Christian brothers and sisters in America ignore the fact that we in Sudan are starving to death?" he asked. Mulholland thought to himself, "I'm glad I don't have to answer that question!" And then, he said, the Holy Spirit tapped him on the shoulder and whispered, "You do." He adds that, as Christians, both he and the Sudanese man pray for daily bread. "For him it is a cry of desperation. For me, it needs to become a vow of generosity."[3]

One of the most moving experiences of my thirty-some years with Bread for the World has been the compassion and generosity of its members, a few of them persons of considerable wealth. I think of Tom White, featured by *Time* magazine as "America's Best Quiet Philanthropist Giver,"[4] who made a fortune in construction. A devout Catholic, he came to have a deep love for Jesus and for giving money to help poor people. Now in his eighties, White has given away almost all of his wealth. "I just really love to give. I just love it," he says.[5] So does joy emerge from sharing what we have.

The Golden Rule, "Do to others as you would have them do to you" (see Matthew 7:12), directly supports such a response. Numerous commentaries on the Gospel of Matthew point out that one can find parallels in rabbinic literature for almost everything Jesus said in the Sermon on the Mount, but not for the Golden Rule, because the sayings that resemble it are without exception stated negatively, along the lines of "What is hateful to you, do not do to another." The same is true of similar teachings in other religions. Only Jesus put it in positive terms. The distinction matters. The negative way tells us to avoid doing harm to others, a rule that seems to be satisfied by inaction. Jesus instead commands doing good. In this way he suggests that the failure to do good is a greater violation of God's will than the doing of evil. Jesus's description of his return in glory (Matthew 25) reinforces this emphasis by telling us that the righteous will be judged by the good they did to the hungry, the destitute, the sick, and the imprisoned, not by the sins they avoided; and the unrighteous will be judged by the good they failed to do.

Greed leads to sins of omission. Trust in God is the first casualty of greed, a terrible loss because trust lies at the heart of our relationship with God. But the second casualty is love. When we are preoccupied with keeping what we have or getting what we do not have, the needs of others fade from our thoughts. It is not so much that we wish them harm as that we have no wishes for them at all. Writer James Fallows observes:

> The way a rich nation thinks about its poor will always be convoluted. The richer people become in general, the easier it theoretically becomes for them to share with people who are left out. But the richer people become, the less they naturally stay in touch with realities of life on the bottom, and the more they naturally prefer to be excited about their own prospects rather than concerned about someone else's.[6]

"I know how very hard it is to be rich and still keep the milk of human kindness," the late archbishop Dom Helder Camara of Recife, Brazil, said.[7]

The poor are not the only ones who suffer. In Jesus's parable, the rich man was afraid of losing control of what he had, so he took steps to keep it, and in doing so, lost everything. By withholding his prosperity from others he prevented himself from becoming rich toward God (Luke 12:16-21). And the rich man who gave Lazarus only scraps from the table was condemned to a fiery torment (Luke 16:19-31). In our own country those who bought and sold slaves warped and twisted themselves by treating people as possessions. The same is true for us if we hang on to our possessions rather than sharing them with people in need. Jesus seems to be telling us that the worst victims are not the oppressed, but the oppressors; not the hungry, but the complacent well-fed. That brings it frighteningly close to home. It should prompt us to pray for daily bread with a bit of fear and trembling, asking God to help us remember who we are in Christ, and to work in us the will to help others.

The Lord's Supper speaks eloquently to the theme of bread for others. As a Passover meal, it has roots in the Exodus and God's provision of *manna* for the Israelites in the wilderness. I have noted that Jesus's feeding of the multitude re-enacted Israel's experience, and the early church connected the feeding with the celebration of the Lord's Supper. The connection was not simply a liturgical repetition of Jesus's blessing, breaking and distribution of the loaves, but his compassion for the hungry. Many recalled that in the messianic age God would feed his people. Today as well the church proclaims the messianic age by being a willing and obedient vessel of God in the fulfillment of this promise. Responding to hunger remains a powerful, authentic sign of the kingdom, prompting at least one theologian, Craig Nessan, to propose that church bodies throughout the world make the ending of world hunger an official confessional position.[8]

Writing to the Christians of Corinth (1 Corinthians 11:17-34) Paul expressed alarm that in celebrating the Lord's Supper, some ate and drank to excess, while poorer brothers and sisters (arriving later, probably because of work obligations) went hungry. The offenders sin against the body and blood of the Lord and invite judgment on themselves, Paul said, by failing to treat fellow believers as part of the body of Christ. The picture is a remarkable snapshot of our world today, with most of us who read this consuming far more than enough, while others throughout the world—many of them sisters and brothers in Christ—go hungry.

Today relief and development agencies report that the cost of a pack of gum can feed a refugee child for a day. The cost of a good shirt would buy fifty pounds of seed corn or school supplies for two children in Africa. The late James P. Grant, director of UNICEF, calculated that, in addition to benefits such as preventing blindness or other disabilities, five hundred dollars spent on child survival saves a child's life. Think of the joy we could give others and ourselves by making radical sharing a part of our celebration of the kingdom.

It is no small thing that Jesus encouraged his followers to practice great generosity to the poor. Such generosity flows from the trust that we place in God for daily bread, and from the hope that we have in Christ.

So measured, how strong is our trust? How great is our hope?

Bread and Justice

To pray that others might receive daily bread is to desire justice, for justice is an expression of love for others. The two go together. They did for Jesus. He not only showed personal compassion, but he also proclaimed justice in the tradition of the prophets. His love of poor people and social outcasts reflected both. When he preached at the synagogue in Nazareth, he read from the prophet

Isaiah, "The Spirit of the Lord is upon me, because he has anointed me to bring good news to the poor. He has sent me to proclaim release to the captives and recovery of sight to the blind, to let the oppressed go free, to proclaim the year of the Lord's favor" (Luke 4:18-19). "The year of the Lord's favor" refers to the year of Jubilee, when slaves were to be freed, debts forgiven, and the land returned to the families who once owned it.

Justice was an intrinsic part of the messianic promise and a mark of the kingdom, so it figured prominently in Jesus's ministry. Quoting Isaiah, the Gospel of Matthew signals that the Lord's chosen servant (Jesus) "will proclaim justice to the nations" and work "till he leads justice to victory" (Matthew 12:18, 20 NIV). Jesus deplored that religious people could get so caught up in the letter of the law that they "neglect justice and the love of God" (Luke 11:42). The righteousness for which Jesus urged us to hunger and thirst (Matthew 5:6) can also be translated "justice." We are to seek the goodness of God that embraces both. But do our prayers and our hopes reflect this?

Justice *now* is linked with justice in its future completeness. Both are expressions of the kingdom. Justice without a future is hopeless. But hope in future justice without efforts to achieve it now is loveless.

A few years after World War II my college roommate, Paul Jersild, and I spent a summer hitchhiking around Western Europe. One of my most indelible memories was the former Nazi concentration camp in Dachau, Germany. I can still see the gas chambers, and ovens where bodies were burned—a literal holocaust. I remember an inscription that read (in

> *You provide enough for all, dear Father. But some get so little, and some of us so much. Oh, that we may become your vessels of love and justice!*

German): "To honor the dead and to admonish the living." On one stone memorial were the words, "Here lie the ashes of ten thousand dead." These were grim reminders of an evil that happened in part because Christians lacked the courage to speak out for public justice.

There were remarkable exceptions, to be sure. But most of those who called themselves Christians feared more for their own safety than for the safety of Jews who were being brutalized and killed. These Christians neither put the kingdom first nor trusted that, if they did, God would take care of them. I wonder if they thought of this when they prayed for daily bread. To be sure, some who did speak up for Jews and assist them paid for it with their lives. Did God not take care of them? Faith that looks to the kingdom measures God's care with a tape much longer than the length of earthly life.

What about us? Each day thirty thousand children from infancy to age five die from malnutrition and disease. Their deaths could be prevented at low cost, but the United States and other industrialized countries have so far not been willing to spend the money and provide the leadership toward a global effort to end widespread hunger. If enough ordinary citizens who bear the name of Christ began urging their national leaders to take such action, it would be done. But we have to be sufficiently aroused in order to arouse our leaders who (like ourselves) are busy with many other things.

Of course, there is a big difference between the slaughter of Jews by the Nazis and our lethargic response to hunger. In one case evil intent drove the killing. In our case it is a matter of neglect. But then Jesus did not say, in his description of the great judgment, "You murdered the hungry, you robbed the naked, you assaulted the poor." He said, in effect, "When I was hungry, naked, and desperate for your help, you ignored me. You passed by on the other side." Neglect.

Let me admit candidly a personal bias on this. My experience as a parish pastor in an economically poor neighborhood of New York City a few decades ago led me to help found and direct Bread for the World, a Christian citizens lobby against hunger. I did so because I began to see the limitations, as well as the importance, of emergency assistance. It became clear to me that in order to make headway against hunger in this country and abroad, we need to enact government policies that are more responsive to hungry people, policies that not only give people immediate relief, but enable them to work their way out of hunger and poverty. I think of charity and justice as two legs. In order to walk, we have to use both of them.

You don't have to be a college graduate to understand this or do something about it. When he was an eighth grader, Nathan Blumenshine got excited about the Jubilee 2000 campaign to forgive the debts of some of the most impoverished countries. So he wrote about it in his school paper, spoke to church youth groups, and organized a junior high dance for which a letter to a member of Congress on the debt issue was the price of admission. Nathan not only influenced Congress, which passed groundbreaking legislation to help those countries; he also impacted the lives of other young people.

Hunger is not the only problem, of course. Violence is another, which should cause us to pray and work diligently for peace. Inadequate health care, education, housing, and employment are among others. All have to do with people's basic needs. The protection of the earth, under threat from global warming, pollution, loss of countless plant and animal species, deforestation, water shortages, and much more is another area that should be of great concern to all who take their God-given stewardship seriously. These are among the issues that have to do with daily bread.

Once when David Beckmann, now president of Bread for the World, was a rising star and gadfly at the World Bank, I asked him, "What is the single most important thing people can do in response to hunger?" I expected a nugget of economic wisdom. Instead he said, "Pray. If we get our prayers straight, everything else follows." It is true. Whatever else it does, bringing concerns to God changes our perspective and our behavior. To pray with Jesus that others may have daily bread is to pray for justice, and then to work for justice that our prayers may be answered.

*   *   *   *

Is it not beyond interesting that our prayer for daily bread, while many go hungry, is followed immediately by a request to God for forgiveness?

9. Forgive As We Forgive—I

One day at age four my son Nathan had gotten into one peck of trouble after another. Tucking him into bed that night, I said I knew the day had been hard for him, but I wanted him to know that I still loved him deeply and had already forgiven him. I said that God loved him even more and had also forgiven him. I told him I needed forgiveness too, every day. I reminded him of Jesus going to the cross for our sins. Then I told him the story of the son who had broken his father's heart by leaving home, doing bad things, and wasting all the money his father had given him until he got so hungry he wished he could eat what the pigs ate. The father waited and waited for his son to return; and then one day he saw his son coming, way off in the distance wearing smelly rags. He ran to his son with tears of joy and threw his arms around him. Then he gave him some clean clothes, and arranged for a big party, because, he said, "This son of mine was dead and is alive again; he was lost and is found!" (Luke 15:11-24). The room fell silent for a moment. Then Nathan said, "You know the first thing I'm gonna do when I get to heaven? I'm gonna run over to God and give him a big hug!"

Forgiveness. How sweet it is!

Nothing is more central to life in the kingdom or to the prayer of Jesus than the forgiveness of sins. As fallen creatures, we can only enter the kingdom of God through forgiveness. Our hope depends on it.

Near death, Henry Thoreau was asked by his aunt, "Henry, have you made your peace with God?" "I didn't know we had ever quarreled," he replied.[1] It is popular with moderns to belittle the idea of sin. One notion is that human nature is basically good, not captive to sin. Another contends that morality is relative, good and bad being fictions that we invent to serve some useful purpose. Still another says we are merely products of our environment, only doing what we do in response to what our surroundings have imposed on us. Such wishful thinking led the famed psychiatrist, Karl Menninger, to write a book, *Whatever Became of Sin?* Human nature is not benign. To deny guilt is to duck one of the ultimate problems that bedevils us. Deep down we know guilt, we feel it, we sense it in our bones, just as we sense the certainty of death. Mental whistling in the dark will not change this. But for those willing to face the unpleasant truth about themselves, the word of forgiveness comes as a cool breeze in the desert heat, as water to a thirsty soul.

When I was growing up, my father cherished Psalm 103, and I came to treasure it as well, because of the way in which it depicts God's love for the oppressed and the love that moves God to forgive us.

> The LORD is merciful and gracious,
>> slow to anger and abounding in steadfast love.
> He will not always accuse,

nor will he keep his anger forever.
He does not deal with us according to our sins,
    nor repay us according to our iniquities.
For as the heavens are high above the earth,
    so great is his steadfast love toward those who fear him;
as far as the east is from the west,
    so far he removes our transgressions from us.
As a father has compassion for his children,
    so the LORD has compassion for those who fear him.
For he knows how we were made;
    he remembers that we are dust (Psalm 103:8-14).

So much for the idea that the Old Testament depicts a vindictive God, and that Jesus came to mollify this angry tyrant. The psalm tells us otherwise. And nothing reveals the heart of God and the depth of God's love so profoundly as the crucifixion of Jesus—the Father's own sacrifice for our sin, the innocent one dying for the guilty to bring us to God.

"Repent, and believe in the good news," Jesus preached (Mark 1:15). He was asking people to turn away from a misdirected life, toward a merciful God. The baptism practiced by John and by Jesus's disciples was a baptism of repentance for the forgiveness of sins (Mark 1:4; Acts 2:38). Jesus's acceptance of poor people and moral outcasts, his eating and drinking with those who were stigmatized as unworthy by religious authorities, put flesh on this teaching. It was as dramatic a sign of the kingdom as was the feeding of the huge crowds.

Friends lowered a paralyzed man through the roof of a crowded house to place him before Jesus for healing—a clever way of getting to the front of the line. The first thing Jesus said to him was, "Take heart, son; your sins are forgiven." Jesus knew what kind of healing the paralytic needed most. Jesus also knew that many people, including perhaps the paralytic, understood his paralysis to be a sign of exceptional sinfulness and God's disfavor. He then told the man to stand up and walk, confirming "that the Son of Man has authority on earth to forgive sins" (Matthew 9:2-8).

Jesus was once invited to dine as a guest in the home of a religious leader, when a woman well known in town for her loose morals intruded and began weeping at Jesus's feet (people reclined as they ate, feet away from the table). After wiping the tears from his feet with her hair and kissing them (imagine your pastor or priest in Jesus's situation!), she poured on them a flask of ointment. The religious leader was visibly upset and thought to himself, "If this man were a prophet, he would know who is touching him and what kind of woman she is—that she is a sinner." So Jesus said to him, "Do you see this woman? I came into your house. You did not give me any water for my feet, but she wet my feet with her tears and wiped them with her hair. You did not give me a kiss, but this woman, from the time I entered, has not stopped kissing my feet. You did not put oil on my head, but she has poured perfume on my feet. Therefore, I tell you, her many sins have been forgiven—as her great love has shown. But whoever has been forgiven little, loves little." Then Jesus said to her, "Your sins are forgiven" (Luke 7:36-48 TNIV).

> *Father, help us to know, and know deeply, how much we have been forgiven, that we may love much.*

Like the story of the prodigal son, this astonishing incident reminds us that sin takes more than one form. The self-righteousness of the religious leader and that of the prodigal's older brother were bigger obstacles to faith than the wanton life of the woman and that of the prodigal himself, because we enter the kingdom through the door of forgiveness. Pride can close that door.

A woman caught in the act of adultery was brought by religious authorities to Jesus. They asked him whether she should be stoned to death, as the law of Moses prescribed. Jesus bent down and began writing on the ground—perhaps listing a few of *their* sins. Then Jesus stood up and said, "Let any one of you who is without sin be the first to throw a stone at her." One by one all went away. Jesus said to her, "Has no one condemned you?" She said, "No one, sir." "Then neither do I condemn you," Jesus declared. "Go now and leave your life of sin" (John 8:2-11 TNIV).[2]

We are in the same boat with all of these sinners, from the religious leader to the adulterous woman; so we pray, "Forgive us our sins." Psalm 51, attributed to King David, said it centuries earlier:

> Have mercy on me, O God,
>   according to your steadfast love;
> according to your abundant mercy
>   blot out my transgressions.
> Wash me thoroughly from my iniquity,
>   and cleanse me from my sin.
>
> Create in me a clean heart, O God,
>   and put a new and right spirit within me.

We need forgiveness for the wrong we have done and for the good that we have left undone, for the sins we know and those of which we are unaware. We pray for a clean heart, even though the extent to which we want a clean heart varies from day to day and moment to moment, and even though we sometimes want its opposite. So we pray not only for a clean heart, but for the desire to have a clean heart. It is not only an admission of what we have done or failed to do, but of who we *are*, persons disposed to sin, instinctively drawn to ourselves more than to God and to others.

When Pope John XXIII, who ushered in the reforms of the Vatican II Council in the 1960s, was told that he had only a few hours to live, he received the bread of holy communion for his final journey. He pointed to the crucifix, which he called the secret of his ministry. "It's there so that I can see it in my first waking moment and before going to sleep. . . . Those open arms have been the program of my pontificate: they mean that Christ died for all, for all. No one is excluded from his love, from his forgiveness."[3]

As We Forgive Others

Now comes the hard part. "Forgive us our sins, *as we forgive those who sin against us.*" The church is not only the fellowship of the forgiven, but it is also the community of those who forgive. To forgive is a hallmark of life in Christ. Forgiving shows that we live with Jesus in hope and participate with him in the kingdom. Not to forgive is to reject the way of the kingdom and cling to the ethic of getting even—an ethic of death. By pardoning us, God wants to heal us, to break down the walls that separate us from God and from one another and rob us of peace. But healing requires that we also pardon others.

Doing so takes courage. Anyone can hate. Anyone can hold a grudge. But releasing hatred and forgiving others takes strength beyond our own. To forgive is truly divine.

Given their natural course, resentment, hatred, and vengeance get caught in an endless cycle of ruin. We see that in ethnic and religious violence. We see it in personal relationships. But in God's new creation forgiveness breaks that cycle. No room for grudges there. God wants us to be at peace, and to make peace with anyone who has sinned against us. Perhaps for you it is a disagreeable co-worker, an offending family member, a friend who has betrayed you, or someone who has harmed your child.

"I can't bring myself to do it," you may be thinking. Perhaps you cannot of your own accord. But God can enable you to do it through Christ, for Christ, and because of Christ. You can look honestly at yourself and at the cross and know, in the depth of your being, how much you have been forgiven, and what a price God paid to forgive you. And then the miracle happens. You, a forgiven sinner, are able to let go of that grudge or that hurt and forgive. You begin to heal.

Forgiving does not excuse or trivialize evil, writes Lewis Smedes in *The Art of Forgiving,* but it is "the only way to heal the wounds of a past we cannot change and cannot forget." When we cling to a hatred—perhaps waiting for an apology that never comes—we give control of ourselves to the person who did us wrong. But "when we forgive, we set someone free—and that person is us."[4] It may set others free as well.

Father J. R. Veneroso, a missionary priest, wrote of the atrocities committed over several decades in Guatemala, "Unless I renounce my urge to retaliate and let go of my grudge, I have placed my happiness in the hands of my adversary." Then on a visit to his home parish in Amsterdam, New York, he went to the home of Mike, his father's best friend when Veneroso was a boy. Mike had suffered a stroke and was in a wheelchair, but he and his father had not spoken to each other for eleven years. Mike's eyes welled up. "Why doesn't your father come to see me anymore?" he asked. So Veneroso asked his father, who fell silent. But his mother explained, "Mike didn't visit your father when he had his operation." "I was in the hospital for two weeks," his father said in self-defense. "Dad, Mike's had a stroke. He's in a wheelchair," Veneroso urged. "Let's stay friends," was his father's way of cutting off debate. "Not if that's the way you treat them," Veneroso snapped back. A few days later his father said, "Come on. Let's go see Mike." Veneroso later wrote, "The fondest memory I have of my father is of him walking behind me into Mike's house and kneeling to bring himself eye level with his friend and the two grown men (no, make that three) crying."[5]

Lou, a friend, told me she has always been overly sensitive to perceived slights. "The good side of being sensitive is that you notice what other people might be feeling," she said, "but it made me too dependent on their reactions to me. Things other people had said or done would show up in my dreams and bounce around in my head like lottery balls. It can tie you knots." She told of a colleague who kept a file in her drawer of personal offenses, so if she ever forgot what someone had done to her, she could bring it to mind again. Lou, however, was determined to do the opposite. "I have gradually learned to let go of those hurts and resentments through prayer and physical activity," she said. "It has been a great relief."

The petition on forgiveness is the only one in Jesus's prayer that explicitly tells us *how* we are to imitate our heavenly Father, and it comes with a solemn warning: "For if you forgive others their trespasses, your heavenly Father will also forgive you; but if you do not forgive others, neither will your Father forgive your trespasses" (Matthew 6:14-15). To be sure, we can do nothing to deserve God's forgiveness. To ask for it is by definition an admission that we fail to measure up. But we can lose God's forgiveness by refusing to forgive others. Willingness to forgive others shows that we truly cherish God's forgiveness, while failure to do so indicates the opposite.

Jesus told the story of a king who forgave an immense, unrepayable debt to an aide who must have engaged in vast mismanagement of the king's affairs. That same man, however, came upon one of his servants who owed him about a hundred days' wages, a substantial but repayable sum. The man seized his servant by the throat and said, "Pay what you owe." The servant begged for time to do so, but the man refused and had him thrown into prison. Others reported this to the king, who summoned that ungrateful aide. "I forgave you all that debt because you pleaded with me," he said. "Should you not have had mercy on your fellow slave, as I had mercy on you?" And in anger his lord handed him over to be tortured until he would pay his entire debt. Jesus added this

> *Father, help us to love as we have been loved, to forgive as we have been forgiven, and to pray for those who sin against us.*

warning: "So my heavenly Father will also do to every one of you, if you do not forgive your brother or sister from your heart" (Matthew 18:23-35). The connection between divine and human forgiveness dare not be broken.

Considering how much we have been forgiven, we are being asked to do something exceedingly small in return. Forgiving others sounds easy, of course, until the idea becomes a specific person who has done us wrong. How hard it suddenly becomes. Forgiveness, however, reflects the heart of God.

Deborah Niyakabirika's son was killed in the massive 1994 genocide slayings in Rwanda. Months later a young man visited her. "I killed your son," he said. "Take me to the authorities and let them deal with me as they will. I have not slept since I shot him. Every time I lie down I see you praying, and I know you are praying for me." She answered, "You are no longer an animal but a man taking responsibility for your actions. I do not want to add death to death," she said. "But I want you to restore justice by replacing the son you killed. I am asking you to become my son. When you visit me, I will care for you." Today that young man is an adopted member of her family.[6]

Large or small, offenses can cause us to harbor resentment. Either way we may have difficulty forgiving. God forgives that sin too, if we *want* it forgiven and are not stubbornly refusing to let go of a grudge or hatred.

I had always taken pride (now there's a warning sign!) in being willing to forgive others, though I never had much to forgive.

Then after thirteen years of marriage, my wife told me she wanted out. I was dismayed. It seemed so unfair. I had been a faithful husband. I was doing God's work in helping to lead Bread for the World. Most upsetting of all, we had adopted (in their infancy) two young boys. I knew that a broken family would do them a huge disservice, and it did. I felt baffled by the emotional and religious changes that my wife was going through, and I certainly did not have enough understanding of our different expectations of the marriage. I was hurt. I was angry. After the divorce I dealt with my feelings by ignoring them and erasing my former wife from my thoughts, unless something came up that re-ignited a smoldering anger. Years later it dawned on me that I wasn't even praying for her, that I didn't *want* to pray for her, and that my buried anger reflected an unwillingness to forgive. It also reflected a refusal to acknowledge my own need to be forgiven for short-comings that I brought to the marriage. I knew that I must let go of my anger and forgive. I have done and continue to do this imperfectly, but doing so has released a burden that was heavier and more dangerous to my soul than I realized.

CBS reported a study (one of many) that showed a striking relationship between good health and people's willingness to forgive. Those who nursed resentments and were unable to forgive others for real or perceived offenses experienced a much higher incidence of high blood pressure, heart disease, and a number of other serious ailments. None of this should surprise us. We are asked to forgive others, however, not for the purpose of better health or longer life, but because it is a way of showing grati- tude to God for the infinitely greater forgiveness we have received through Christ.

We are asked to forgive, not forget. Of course, to say "I can forgive but I can't forget," often means "I don't really forgive." However, if a baby-sitter neglects or abuses your child, God does not ask you to forget the offense. You are not required to put your child in the hands of that baby sitter again. A battered wife is not required to return to danger. Forgiving someone is not the same as tolerating sin, but facing it for the awful thing it is, and in spite of that releasing personal hatred.

You can hate the sin but love the sinner. That's exactly what God does. C. S. Lewis thought this a silly idea until it occurred to him that "there was one man to whom I had been doing this all my life—namely myself. However much I might dislike my own cowardice or conceit or greed, I went on loving myself. There had never been the slightest difficulty about it. In fact the very reason why I hated the things was that I loved the man."[7]

Forgiveness does not rule out corrective steps to protect people or change behavior; but corrective action should serve the purpose of helping others, not that of getting even.

This petition invites us to listen to God and reflect on the Father's mercy to us. Because we are truly forgiven, we need not dwell on past sins or wallow in guilt. Instead we find refreshment in knowing that the slate is clean and we can move forward. But we must also ask: Whom do I need to forgive?

10. Forgive As We Forgive—II

Helen Joynes, a member of my church, told me that when she was a little girl she learned that her grandmother and her grandmother's sister had not spoken to each other for years, though both considered themselves devout believers. "Grandma," she asked, "why don't you and Aunt Lena talk to each other?" Her grandmother, caught by surprise, thought for a minute and then said with some embarrassment, "I don't remember." Alarmed by this inquiry and the realization of how the grudge was felt even by Helen, the two elderly sisters became reconciled.

Much of what Jesus said about forgiveness was directed at the way in which we are to accept one another as sisters and brothers in the faith. Jesus said that if a fellow believer has sinned against us, we should first privately seek reconciliation with that person, and if that fails, attempt with others in the church to reach the offender. This prompted Peter to ask, "Lord, how many times shall I forgive someone who sins against me? Up to seven times?" Jesus answered him, "I tell you, not seven times, but seventy-seven times" (Matthew 18:21-22 TNIV). Forgiveness doesn't keep score. Just as we never stop needing and receiving God's forgiveness, we are never to stop forgiving others.

This applies to someone who offends repeatedly. But I think it also applies to a single offense that has hurt deeply and is particularly hard to forgive, one for which resentment may keep returning (as it did for me), and for which we may need to come again and again before God and ask for the ability to forgive.

Even more striking than specific biblical texts urging believers to forgive one another is the premium that Jesus and the New Testament writers place on love and unity in Christ. During supper on the eve of his execution, Jesus took a basin of water and a towel, and washed his disciples' feet—the role of a lowly servant. Then he told them that they should wash one another's feet. "I have set you an example, that you also should do as I have done to you," he said (John 13:1-15). Then he gave them a "new commandment, that you love one another." What made the commandment new was that they were to love "as I have loved you" (John 13:34). Sacrificial love. Self-giving love. Later that evening, in prayer, Jesus asked his Father "that they [my followers] may be one, as we are one . . . so that the world may know that you have sent me . . ." (John 17:21-23).

One of the most exciting developments in my lifetime was the Vatican II Council during the 1960s, which opened windows for change within the Roman Catholic Church. I remember the joy, for me as a Lutheran parish pastor and for the congregation I served, to discover how much we had in common with our neighboring Catholic congregation, and how much we could learn from each other. We cherished our unity in Christ as the treasure it was, despite differences. I think we experienced mutual forgiveness, though it was never put that way, for having ignored each other and gone our separate ways.

But the main focus in the New Testament is on life *within* the local congregation. The apostle Paul constantly urged young churches to show love and unity. He said that distinctions between Jews and gentiles, slaves and free people, male and female no longer mattered, "for all of you are one in Christ Jesus" (Galatians 3:28). He urged the believers in Philippi to serve one another humbly, in the manner of Jesus (Philippians 2:1-5). He told the Christians of Rome to avoid those who cause divisions in the church (Romans 16:17). And his classic chapter on love (1 Corinthians 13) is addressed to Christians who had split into factions.

Perhaps nowhere else are the themes of unity and forgiveness more eloquently put than in Ephesians, which tells us to be "eager to maintain the unity of the Spirit in the bond of peace. (Ephesians 4:3 RSV). We are to "be kind to one another, tenderhearted, forgiving one another, as God in Christ forgave you," (4:32) to "be imitators of God, as beloved children. And walk in love, as Christ loved us" (5:1-2), and to "be subject to one another out of reverence for Christ" (5:21).

Reinforcing all of this was the way in which Jesus brazenly ignored the distinctions that had created a religious and social caste system. He outraged the authorities by associating with those who were regarded as unworthy or ceremonially unclean—poor people, gentiles, lepers, the lame and blind, tax collectors, and women (including a Samaritan, another with menstrual bleeding, and evidently a few prostitutes). His love, his kingdom, was open to all. Jesus was tough on sinners who refused to forgive other sinners. "He saw the laughable incongruity of people who need to be forgiven a lot turning their backs on people who need a little forgiving from them."[1] This sent a clear message to the disciples about the kind of community they were to become. But how many of our churches today welcome outcasts the way Jesus did? "They [outcasts] think of church as a place to go *after* you have cleaned up your act, not before," writes Philip Yancey. "They think of morality, not grace."[2]

Community in Christ is based on God's acceptance of us and our acceptance of each other. It is easy to forget that we are called to love and serve one another as we engage in the mission God has given us. Disagreements are bound to occur. We can either build walls with them and reflect the brokenness of the world, or we can forgive one another and together seek the unity that is ours in Christ. We need to pray fervently for this.

Love Your Enemies

If love and forgiveness are hallmarks of the way that brothers and sisters in Christ regard each other, they are also—astoundingly—the hallmarks of our regard for those who hate and persecute us. "Father, forgive them; for they know not what they do" (Luke 23:34 KJV), Jesus cried out on the cross—the most crisp and poignant exegesis of the crucifixion ever, because he was enacting the very thing that he declared. His words were echoed in the dying prayer of Stephen, the first Christian martyr, as stones crushed the life out of his body: "Lord, do not hold this sin against them" (Acts 7:60).

In his letter to the Christians at Rome the apostle Paul—who had approvingly witnessed Stephen's stoning—notes how rare it is for someone to die for a righteous person, though it happens. "But God proves his love for us in that while we still were sinners Christ died for us." By doing so Jesus not only demonstrated God's love, but reconciled us to God "while we were enemies" (Romans 5:8-10).

It is in this context that words of Jesus from the Sermon on the Mount take on a powerful meaning for us. The way of the world, Jesus notes, is to hate your enemy. But if you only love those who love you, and are good only to those who are good to you, and friendly only to your friends, Jesus asked, how is that different from the way in which crooks and unbelievers behave? "But I say to you, Love your enemies and pray for those who persecute you . . ." (Matthew 5:44). We should, he said, follow the example of our Father in heaven who gives the sun and the rain to the good and bad alike—an example that Jesus magnified on the cross.

We are to *pray* for those who mistreat us. That goes with the territory of love. Anger, which easily slips into hatred, blocks our prayers, as I discovered. But one of the best ways of turning aside anger and hatred is to pray for those who have done us wrong. When we pray for them, we begin to think of them in a different way, no longer as enemies, because we are asking God for their physical and spiritual well-being. Even a minor annoyance, which may cause us to resent and mentally diminish others—say, neighborhood kids who make noise or trample the grass—can be countered by the prayer of love. It is hard to resent people if we see them through the eyes of Christ. Praying for them will change us, and it may also change them.

After the destruction of the World Trade Center buildings on September 11, 2001, I was dismayed to learn that one of the victims was Celeste Torres Victoria, whom I had baptized forty years earlier when she was about two years old. Celeste was one of five young children, whose mother was a single parent on welfare. When I first visited them their situation appeared almost hopeless to me. But they became active in the church, the mother eventually got a college degree, and each of the children has done well in a chosen career. Celeste became a media specialist who happened to be attending a meeting on the 105th floor of one of the buildings when the terrorists struck. It was a terrible blow to the family. About a year after Celeste's death, I asked her sister Dawn about her feelings toward the terrorists. "To tell you the truth, I don't think about that," she said. "We just remember Celeste and try to get on with our lives."

Emmett Till, a fourteen-year-old boy from Chicago, was brutally killed by Klansmen in Mississippi in 1955 while visiting relatives. He was said to have spoken disrespectfully to or whistled (two versions) at a white woman. After his body arrived in Chicago, his mother had the coffin opened so the public could see his mangled face. It created a national sensation and built public opinion for civil rights. In her old age Till's mother was alone and in a wheelchair. Her son, had he lived, might have been there to care for her. But she told a caller, "I have not spent one minute hating."[3]

The apostle Paul would have understood. At first he persecuted Christians, and then was himself persecuted for the faith that he once opposed. But, he said, "forgetting what lies behind and straining forward to what lies ahead, I press on toward the goal for the prize of the heavenly call of God in Christ Jesus" (Philippians 3:13-14). He had no time for being captive to hatred or self-pity, only the freedom of forgiveness—his own and that which he extended to others.

Judge Not

The counterpart to "Forgive us as we forgive" is "Judge not and you will not be judged." We pray for that as well in this petition, because we are called upon to confess our own sins, not the sins of others. Judgment belongs to God alone. Jesus put it bluntly:

> Do not judge, or you too will be judged. For in the same way you judge others, you will be judged, and with the measure you use, it will be measured to you.
>
> Why do you look at the speck of sawdust in someone else's eye and pay no attention to the plank in your own eye? How can you say, 'Let me take the speck out of your eye,' when all the time there is a plank in your own eye? You hypocrite, first take the plank out of your own eye, and then you will see clearly to remove the speck from the other person's eye (Matthew 7:1-5 TNIV).

I know people, as you doubtlessly do, who have a habit of criticizing others. Quick to complain if they sense that they are being treated less well than someone else, they are alert to the shortcomings of people around them—family members, co-workers, church members, neighbors. They tend to be slow to thank others but quick to set them straight. But here we are, judging them, though none of us is immune from this tendency!

I've noticed that we pay the price of which Jesus warned. When we judge others, that judgment comes back to haunt us in the form of self-judgment. We inescapably impose on ourselves the judgment we heap on others. If we cannot be merciful to others, we will not in the depths of our heart be merciful to ourselves. When we tear them down, we subconsciously tear down ourselves for our own behavior as well. But Jesus was not offering a bit of useful psychology. He was warning that the judgment of others invites the judgment of God, just as failure to forgive others invites God to withhold forgiveness from us.

Our judgments are always based on very limited information and understanding, while God's judgment is not. We often err, but God does not. I easily forget that very different circumstances have shaped others, and advantages that I have had are not remotely like the crushed hopes that may haunt them. I cannot know how I would respond, given the circumstances they face. In addition, my judgments reflect cultural biases that are often at sharp variance with God's view of things. In the four Gospels we see Jesus repeatedly turning the world's values upside down (that is, rightside up). The Pharisees were models for the religious life, not Zaccheus the tax collector. The rich man would have been admired and honored, not Lazarus the disgustingly sick and smelly beggar who loitered at his gate.

I need to see others as God sees them. If I am rude to a beggar, a woman of the street, or someone who doesn't fit in, I insult God, for they are God's children. I insult you, for they are your brother and sister. And I insult myself, for we are equals.

Of course, it is necessary for us to make assessments of others, say, in choosing where to work or whom to vote for, in guiding our children toward suitable friends, or in deciding who should take care of the house or the kids while we are away. But these should always be considered provisional calls, not final determinations about the character of others. I would hate to admit how often I have been wrong in sizing people up, only to be subsequently surprised. I have made mistakes in hiring and in not hiring people. I have written off some as being of little consequence and learned years later how much they accomplished, what good they have done, and how their lives have shamed my own. These things remind me how prone to fault our judgment is, and that even when tentative judgments must be made, they should be made in a humble spirit, and never at the expense of another's humanity.

Not judging others, like forgiving others, should not be confused with being wishy-washy about sin. God's holiness and the judgment that God rightly exercises against sin must be viewed with utmost respect. If we do not take sin seriously, God's forgiveness seems easy and shallow, not at all the awesome, life-transforming gift that alone can save us. As Jesus said, "Whoever has been forgiven little loves little" (Luke 7:47 TNIV). So the point is not to get soft on sin and water down forgiveness, but to be so overwhelmed by God's mercy toward us that we become merciful to others.

Restorative Justice

Matthew and Luke present the petition on forgiveness in different ways:

Forgive us our *debts,* as we also have forgiven our *debtors* (Matt. 6:12).

Forgive us our *sins,* for we ourselves forgive everyone *indebted to us* (Luke 11:4).

"Sins" and "sins against us" probably convey the overall meaning best, because in the Aramaic language of Jesus, the word for *sin* and *debt* was the same. *Sin* was almost surely the main idea here. Yet devout Jews with an understanding of the Old Testament tradition of debt forgiveness every seven years (Deuteronomy 15) would have associated Jesus's words about forgiveness of sins with debt forgiveness as well. The connection here between forgiveness of sins and social justice is pretty clear, and would fit Jesus's instruction elsewhere to "love your enemies, do good, and lend, expecting nothing in return" (Luke 6:35).

The point of the petition, in any case, is that God wants to restore broken lives and relationships, and wants us to do the same. This intention of God is shown in two distinct ways: by the grace of forgiveness, and by the law.

The family is a good example of a social unit that may reflect both. If the family is Christian, the home should function as a place where the gospel is taught, the love of Christ shared, and family members forgive one another. This reflects God's rule by grace. But the same family will also express God's rule by law. Parents will exercise authority, set ground rules, and discipline offenders. In such a family the law has a protective but coercive function, though its purpose is ultimately care and restoration. A family in which coercion becomes more prominent than forgiveness is in trouble.

The government operates under God by rule of law, not by the gospel. The state has the authority and the duty to establish public justice. However, when the state imprisons someone, say, for defrauding or injuring another, the injured party, if she or he is a Christian, may be obligated by faith to express both aspects of God's rule: first, by testifying against the criminal, and second, by praying for that person—replacing hatred with forgiveness. The latter will not come easily or quickly in all likelihood, and it may require the constancy of a lifetime to lift up one's feelings, along with the need of the offender, to God.

Randy, the son of a former colleague of mine on the Bread for the World staff, spent twenty years on death row in Nebraska. Under the influence of multiple drugs, he killed one of his best friends, Janet, and her friend Vicki—a crime of which he has no memory—while they were staying in a Friends Meeting House (Quaker Church). Janet and Randy had grown up together as members of another Friends Meeting. Randy's death sentence was set aside on a technicality and he was re-sentenced to life in prison, after the prosecutor declined to further pursue the death penalty. Clearly people in the community and state, and probably the prosecutor, were swayed by repeated appeals from Janet's family (which still worships weekly with Randy's family) and from the daughter and husband Vicki left behind not to impose the death penalty. Though devastated by the murders, they sought healing in forgiveness, not vengeance.[4]

In Randy's case personal forgiveness influenced criminal justice. The purpose of the cross was to reconcile the world to God. Reconciliation, not punishment, is God's ultimate purpose. In that lies a lesson. The U.S. criminal justice system is overwhelmingly aimed at punishment. Retribution, not restoration, is the goal. Consequently, prisoners are often treated so inhumanely that they become more hardened. Even the victims of their crimes may be given scant consideration, their needs readily sacrificed to the purpose of convicting and punishing offenders. Something is wrong with this picture.

Most prisoners are either school drop-outs (many of them functionally illiterate) and/or were addicted to drugs. Yet opportunities in prison for obtaining an education, job skills, or getting into a drug rehabilitation program are very limited. "Lock 'em up and throw away the key" is the popular attitude. But when prison terms have been served and prisoners released, they are usually ill-equipped to find their way in society. Consequently, most return to crime and to prison, a far more costly outcome than preparing prisoners for a constructive role in life.

Ruban, an eighteen-year old who lives around the corner from me, was arrested a few months ago for armed robbery. It was his first offense. He let a few "friends" talk him into something stupid and evil. Now he will spend years in prison. I wonder what will happen to this impressionable young man there. Will he be molded for a criminal future, or will he be prepared to make a new start in life?

Justice can be wisely tempered with mercy for the purpose of restoring relationships and mending society. The Truth and Reconciliation Commission chaired by Archbishop Desmond Tutu gave amnesty to those who publicly confessed crimes committed under South Africa's apartheid regime, bringing some measure of healing to that country. The generous treatment of Germany and Japan by the United States and its allies after World War II paved the way for friendly democracies that have added immeasurably to a more peaceful and prosperous world. That does not make such action gospel, but experiencing God's forgiveness may motivate those who govern to aim for public justice that restores.

As this petition shows, Jesus is calling us to live in a radically new way. The mission that Jesus has given us is to begin practicing now the life that is ours in God's eternal kingdom. We are to be peacemakers, reconcilers, healers, people of mercy. Our purpose is never to get even, but to restore what is broken. That applies to every aspect of life, from personal relationships to public justice. This gives us more than enough to think and pray about and do each day.

Instead of grousing about that unfriendly cashier or colleague at work, we can make it our aim to arouse their friendliness with our own.

Instead of returning anger with anger at home, we can offer kindness and prayers.

Instead of seeking public vengeance on wrongdoers, we can seek a justice that heals because its toughness is tempered with help.

That is the way of Jesus. It is a project for a lifetime.

11. Deliver Us from Evil

"I can resist anything except temptation," the playwright Oscar Wilde once said.

We laugh because he pokes fun at himself about a weakness that all of us share.

Unfortunately that weakness is often fatal. It reflects a struggle for our allegiance that goes on each day deep within our hearts. It is part of a cosmic drama. We are in danger so grave that God alone can rescue us. So we pray, "Lead us away from temptation, and deliver us from evil."

I detect a tone of desperation here that is missing from other petitions in Jesus's prayer. It reflects the realism of faith. No papering over the evil that abounds in the world, no soothing of ourselves and others with comforting thoughts about our innate goodness, but instead a recognition of the depths to which humans can sink and the faithlessness of which we ourselves are capable.

Our struggle is part of a cosmic drama, but allow me to admit that I don't understand this well. According to the biblical witness something is happening that reaches far beyond our world. Much is at stake for all of us, and God cares passionately about the outcome. It is a mind-boggling thought that in this unbelievably vast universe we tiny humans on this little speck of that universe are of huge importance to God. But this is not a bedtime story in which a fairy godmother waves her wand and turns the frog into a prince. It is rather a real conflict in which our destiny is intertwined with the destiny of all creation.

The Apostle Paul says that God's creation is now subjected to futility, groaning as though in labor pains of childbirth. It is eager to be set free from its bondage to decay and obtain freedom and glory when the children of God are made fully new in the resurrection. Not only we, Paul says, but the whole creation will be made new (Romans 8:18-23). So God's triumph in Christ over evil, though conclusive, is far from complete. It is like a war in which the decisive battle has been won, the outcome assured, but fierce fighting continues.

We get another glimpse of this in Ephesians. "For our struggle is not against enemies of blood and flesh, but against the rulers, against the authorities, against the cosmic powers of this present darkness, against the spiritual forces of evil in the heavenly places" (6:12). These cosmic powers are at war with God. We can recognize this not only within ourselves but also in the way power is exercised in the world. Tyrannical and corrupt regimes reflect this; but so do injustices within the best of democracies, where people may go hungry despite food surpluses and economic prosperity. The evil that we contend with personally pervades all political and social structures. The struggle that goes on within us is connected to the culture in which we live. We are caught in a web of evil, and so we cry out, "Deliver us!"

Because of Christ, however, we do not despair. The Father, who has given us hope in Jesus, does deliver us from evil and lets us participate now in his everlasting reign. At the last day our deliverance will be complete. That is the thrust not only of this petition, but of the entire prayer.

"Lead Us Not into Temptation"

Christians are often puzzled by the line, "Lead us not into temptation." Would God lead us into temptation? Although the words seem wrong, their intent is clarified by the companion line, "but deliver us from evil." Once again we have a Hebrew parallelism. In this case Jesus emphasizes the point by casting it first in a negative and then in a positive way. The second line is strengthened by its contrast with the first, so the overall meaning is quite clear.

Still, a puzzle remains. In distinction to Matthew's version (6:9-13), Luke's shortened form of the prayer (11:2-4) adds no clarifying line, but simply ends with "Lead us not into temptation." Why these words if, as the church teaches and the epistle of James clearly states (1:13-14), God tempts no one?

One explanation lies in the language that Jesus spoke. The Aramaic language does not have an exact equivalent of "lead," but would have used "cause to go." In that case the "not" could be inserted so as to make the petition read, "Cause us *not* to go into temptation." That is probably the way it was said by Jesus, and only when translated into Greek did the confusion arise.[1] So a better reading would be, "Lead us away from temptation."

Another explanation is that the Greek word *temptation* can also be translated "test" or "trial," a more apt meaning in the view of many scholars. (Based on this, the New Revised Standard Version reads, "Do not bring us to the time of trial.")

A translation that combines both of the above explanations is used in many churches: "*Save us* from the time of trial."

Whatever the best translation, I think Jesus meant to encompass the meaning of both "test" and "temptation," closely related as they are. Whichever word is used, it should not be thought of as a hankering to sleep late or eat an extra dessert (though these are not always trivial), but rather as a thing that threatens to undermine our faith and bring it crashing down. When a public confession of faith might mean persecution or even death, this is a particularly urgent concern.

Matthew writes that "Jesus was *led by the Spirit* into the desert to be tempted by the devil" (4:1 NIV). A bit later Matthew records the petition (as usually prayed), "Lead us not into temptation" (6:13 NIV). So perhaps we are being asked to pray, "Do not lead us into [or: Save us from] the kind of extreme testing that Jesus faced."

Consistent with this, the "evil" from which we need to be rescued can also be translated "the evil one," meaning the devil or Satan. We pray that Satan would not be allowed to ruin our life with God. So the petition might be translated, "Do not put us to the test [that threatens our faith], but rescue us from the evil one."

I speak of the devil or Satan with hesitation because we have stereotyped Satan in ways that invite ridicule—as a creature with horns and a pitchfork, or one to be blamed for all personal and social irresponsibility ("the devil made me do it"). Satan is then reduced to a laughable cartoon or made a convenient substitute for serious thought, repentance, and constructive action. But evil as a personal force that each of us is intimately acquainted with, that each of us has to contend with, and that is able to seduce us when left to our own devices—this I believe. I can understand evil power, acting like a lion looking for prey (1 Peter 5:8) or a deceiver with attractive promises to lure us from our hope and purpose in life. I see evidence of such evil in a wide array of injustices. These forms of evil are confirmed by my own experience and today's news.

Temptation with a Capital "T"

It is the Big Test, the Big Temptation, we are taught especially to fear in this prayer. The classic examples are the temptation of Adam and Eve, and its mirror opposite, Jesus's own temptation. In the Genesis account of the fall, the serpent tells Eve that if she and Adam eat the forbidden fruit, "your eyes will be opened, and you will be like God, knowing everything."[2] An awesome prospect! The irony was that they had been created in the image of God. Their reach for equality with God corrupted rather than enhanced that likeness for the human family. Jesus, however, was a new and strikingly opposite human prototype,[3]

> who, though he was in the form of God,
> did not regard equality with God
> as something to be exploited,
> but emptied himself,
> taking the form of a slave,
> being born in human likeness.
> And being found in human form,
> he humbled himself
> and became obedient to the point of death—
> even death on a cross.
> Therefore God also highly exalted him . . .
> (Philippians 2:6-9).

Following his baptism and before beginning his public ministry, Jesus fasted in the desert for forty days and nights (recalling Israel's forty years of testing in the wilderness), during which time the tempter assailed him. The gospels then report a struggle for the heart of Jesus, an attempt to get Jesus to use the power he had for personal advantage. The account belongs in the context of what the gospels show to be an overwhelming desire among the people of Israel for a Messiah who would liberate them from oppressive Roman rule. So, for example, when Satan showed Jesus the kingdoms of the world in all their splendor, it was as though he said, "Look, here's the world as it really is, governed by the powerful and given to me. I'm the one who controls it, for as you can plainly see, might makes right on this earth. You can have it all—not merely a piece of it, but all of it. Just give me your allegiance and the power and the glory of the world will be yours." This was the insistent call to fulfill the dreams of the people and become their earthly liberator.[4]

Though compacted in the gospel accounts as one story, the temptation or testing of Jesus must have occurred repeatedly throughout his ministry, for Luke writes that the devil "departed from him until an opportune time" (4:13), and at the Last Supper Jesus tells his disciples, "You are those who have stood by me in my trials" (22:28). Clearly the greatest test of all came when the crucifixion drew near and Jesus, overwhelmed with sorrow and dread, threw himself to the ground in the Garden of Gethsemane. "Oh, no, Father, not this!" must have raced through his mind. Sweating profusely he prayed that, if possible, the cup of horrible suffering might be removed from him. Yet he said, "Your will be done" (Matthew 26:42).

> Father, the birds of temptation fly overhead. Please do not let them nest in our hair!

The disciples faced their own test. When Jesus told them they would desert him, Peter protested that he would die first—and the other disciples chimed in with the same vow. Jesus knew better. "Simon, Simon, listen! Satan has demanded to sift all of you like wheat, but I have prayed for you that your own faith may not fail; and you, when once you have turned back, strengthen your brothers" (Luke 22:31-32). By calling him "Simon" instead of "Peter," Jesus reminded him of his weakness and that by himself Peter was no rock, just chaff blown away from the wheat.

Then in anguish before and during his praying in the garden, he urged his disciples, "Stay awake and pray that you may not come into the time of trial" (Matthew 26:41). But they slept. And soon they fled.

From all of this we understand temptation or testing as posing a grave danger to our faith and our faithfulness. At stake is our place in God's family, the privilege of having God as our *Abba*, and our life in the kingdom.

Lower Case Temptations

If temptation is seen as a crisis in which our faith is threatened—the primary, though not the only way in which the word is used in the New Testament—we should not conclude that lesser temptations or tests are of little consequence. Vices that seem deceptively small to us may gradually ensnare us, so the line between faith-threatening and non-faith-threatening temptations is far from exact.

If we are faced with persecution and danger to our life or well-being, at least it is clear to us that the stakes are high. Many in our own day have had to conform to the culture or suffer dire consequences for their faith. There were more Christian martyrs in the twentieth century, it has been said, than in all the previous nineteen centuries combined.

But what if the stakes are *low*? What if we have to choose between conforming or missing out on some fun? Fitting in or being viewed as an oddball? No big deal, just a little discomfort. What do we do then? Is lack of courage in the face of trivial costs any less deplorable than lack of courage in the face of great danger? And if we fail small tests, what makes us think we would pass the big ones? When I reflect on this and consider my own record, I pray the petition more fervently.

Consider the influences that surround us and the way in which they shape our thoughts, attitudes, and behavior. So pervasive are these influences that we may accept them almost unconsciously. The affluent life, freedom of choice, and endless opportunities and enjoyments begin to define our aspirations. The purposes of God for us and for our children get pushed aside, and compassion for others is neglected. We may not even think of this as a test of faith.

In my own case, or so I perceive, it has always been seemingly small temptations that undermine my faith—termites rather than tyrants, subtle rather than brazen challenges. Sometimes it is the tug of pride, sometimes a bit of self-righteousness, sometimes the desire to be well liked. Sometimes it has led to foolish decisions because I insisted on my own way and failed to give place to God. Sometimes it has been attachment to material things that caused me to be forgetful of those who lack bare necessities. Sometimes it is time and abilities not well used, treasures buried rather than invested. In short, I do not have enough trust in God and what God could do through me if I were more courageous and faithful. For this reason I need to pray, "Lead us away from temptation, and deliver us from evil."

I recently read a front-page newspaper article featuring the faith of Joe Gibbs, coach of the (insensitively named) Washington Redskins. He has been influential in attracting many to faith in Christ, mostly because of his example. His life exudes integrity and invites respect. "I'm constantly seeking God's direction in my life because I've made so many mistakes,"[5] he said. That's consoling if you are as mistake-prone as I am.

So, deliver us from . . .

• Mistaking our wishes for God's will
• Judging others
• Holding a grudge

- Forgetting to be friendly
- Wasting time
- Engaging in gossip
- Remaining silent when God or neighbor is ridiculed
- Spending generously on ourselves while others starve
- Passively accepting other injustices

You can make your own list. The point of this is not that we should nourish guilt, but that we need at all times to pray for the courage to live fully and faithfully for God. In this petition we beg God to help us through anything that may cause us to neglect our purpose in life.

The good news is that because we are forgiven, each day we can forget the sins that lie behind and press forward in Christ Jesus. The good news also is that Jesus gives us such a positive and purpose-filled life that, as we grab hold of it, temptation loses much of its luster.

Adversity

When I pray, "Deliver us from evil," I include people on my daily prayer list who face adversity. Some are sick and dying, some grieve, some struggle with gathering disabilities, some are in prison, and some for other reasons have had dreams shattered and hopes crushed. Around the world, hunger, poverty, disease, violence, slavery, natural calamities, accidents, and betrayal take their toll. Injustice lies behind and compounds much of this awful reality. Each day the news brings to our attention a heartrending sample of people who suddenly experience incredible pain or sadness.

When we have to walk through the valley of death's darkness or face some other calamity, we may be put to the test, tempted to doubt or despair and cry out, "Where is God?" The first funeral I conducted was the death of an infant girl, the only child of a young couple. I could hardly bear to see their sorrow, though they showed more faith than I could imagine having under the circumstances. Temporal sense made no sense to me.

Martin Luther's four-year-old daughter, Anastasia, was jabbering about Christ, angels, and heaven. Luther said, "My dear child, if only we could hold fast to this faith."

"Why, Papa," she said, "don't you believe it?"

Luther commented, "Christ has made the children our teachers. I am chagrined that although I am ever so much a doctor [teacher], I still have to go to the same school with Hans and Magdalena, for who among us can understand the full meaning of this word of God, 'Our Father who art in heaven'? . . . And while I am affirming this faith, my Father suffers me to be thrown into prison, drowned, or beheaded. Then faith falters and in weakness I cry, 'Who knows whether it is true?'"[6]

Luther was periodically assailed by depression and doubt, but he also believed that it made him a better theologian, driving him again and again to trust in Christ. I do not believe that God is the author of depression, but I believe from what I have seen that God can use suffering to awaken us, strengthen our trust, deepen our compassion, and help us respond to the suffering of others. "If we see the world with eyes that have wept," writes Deborah Smith Douglas, "we may be ready to enter more deeply, with God, into the suffering of the broken world."[7]

A few months ago, as I write this, Walt Rast, a cherished friend from seminary days who became an Old Testament scholar and archeologist, died from a malignant brain tumor. When I learned that he had an incurable cancer, I wrote to him. His reply included the following: "Suzanna [his wife] and I have taken on this challenge by 'redeeming the time' as Paul puts it. We've rediscovered the new beginning in Christ. Rather than be pulled down in sadness, we've taken hold of the resurrection life—living each day in new awareness of God's gifts, in creation, in our family and friends, a new and deepened sensitivity to all the suffering people in the world. . . . So we're doing well. God is good to us." In ways such as this God delivers us from evil even in the face of anguish.

Above my desk I have placed these words of Lucia from Alessandro Manzoni's novel, *The Betrothed*: "He who gave you so much joy is everywhere; and he never disturbs the happiness of his children, except to prepare for them a surer and greater happiness."

Jesus's own ministry connects the relationship between suffering and evil. His healing, especially the casting out of demons, was a signal that God is at work to overcome the forces of evil. The gospels depict Jesus's healing of the demon-possessed as a confrontation with Satan and evidence of the power of God. "If I drive out demons by the finger of God, then the kingdom of God has come to you," Jesus said (Luke 11:20 NIV).

Jesus rejected the popular assumption that illness, disability, or untimely death indicated special guilt and God's judgment. When Jesus healed the man who had been blind from birth, the disciples asked, "Rabbi, who sinned, this man or his parents, that he was *born* blind?" Jesus replied, "Neither . . . ; he was born blind so that God's works might be revealed in him" (John 9:1-3)—revealed, that is, when Jesus restored his sight. That does not answer the question of blindness that is *not* cured, but it tells us that whatever our condition, God has a far higher purpose in mind for us—that we see with eyes of faith and receive the kingdom.

> Father, help us so to anchor
> our hope in the kingdom,
> and have such joy and purpose
> in Christ, that other paths
> will not attract us.
> But when they do, deliver us.

Fending Off Evil

Luther, illustrating the difference between temptation and sin, said that we cannot keep birds from flying over our heads, but we can prevent them from nesting in our hair.

The birds do fly. Whether by some form of seduction or suffering, we are constantly being tested. "The wonderful thing about God's schoolroom," wrote Charles Swindoll, "is that we get to grade our own papers. . . . [God] tests us so *we* can discover how well we're doing."[8] Although God does not tempt us, God does test us so that our faith may increase. As a kite rises in the face of the wind, so faith grows stronger by being challenged. We pray in this petition that the kite of our faith may rise against the wind of temptation and adversity, but not be destroyed or carried away by it.

"Deliver us from evil" is not a petition for the proud who feel little need for help, nor for the cowardly who, like water, seek the easiest path. It is for those who want to be strong and yet know how quickly they crumble when assaulted by the cunning of the tempter, apart from the strength that God alone gives. And sometimes it is only after crumbling, as Peter did in his denial of Jesus, that we are forced to recognize our weakness and see our desperate need of help.

God's help is crucial. The petition does not ask us to become preoccupied with ourselves and with our weaknesses. Its intent is to turn us to God for deliverance. We look to the Father's strength, not our weakness; to life in God's eternal kingdom, not the culture of death. That is the whole point of the Lord's Prayer.

We do not overcome evil by concentrating on overcoming evil. We overcome evil with good. We fight wrong desires best by replacing them with the higher desire for God. Hearts set on the kingdom and on the mission of Jesus give evil no lasting opportunity.

"Every temptation is an opportunity to do good," writes Rick Warren.[9] I like that, because it reminds me that in Christ I can defy evil and live as a child of the kingdom.

The example of those whose faith has shone with particular brightness can serve us well in this regard. I think of John Bosco, a little known nineteenth century Italian priest in the city of Turin. He came from a very poor family, and early in life felt a calling to help boys who were social castoffs and street urchins. He engaged them in sports, helped educate and train them, brought them into the church, and over the years led thousands of boys to Jesus.[10]

Lives such as his give us a glimpse of the kingdom and stir in us the desire to be more fully a part of Jesus's mission. The tradition within the Roman Catholic and Eastern churches of finding inspiration from the lives of the saints (such as Fr. John Bosco) has much to commend itself in this regard. So do the lives of many close at hand if we are willing to look: the widow who faithfully volunteers to help at every opportunity; that teen-ager so energetic and eager to give her life to Jesus; the family, struggling to make ends meet but full of love and good works.

This petition appropriately comes last because, whatever its form, temptation is an appeal to sin against all the other petitions. The best way to fend it off is:

- to be filled with joy in knowing God as our beloved Abba;
- to honor God's holy name in all that we think and do;
- to seek first the Father's kingdom and will for us;
- to trust God for every need, and gratefully tend to the needs of others; and
- to forgive and be forgiven.

When we are alive to the presence of God in this way, trusting in God's goodness even when we do not feel it, and setting our ultimate hope in heaven, there will be much to celebrate and little room for evil to gain a foothold.

12. The Kingdom, Power, and Glory Are Yours

First, a little detour.

If we go by the earliest recorded texts of Matthew and Luke, the prayer is already finished. In Luke it ends, "Lead us not into temptation." In Matthew, the final phrase is "but deliver us from evil." The church has combined distinctive features of the prayer from each gospel, so today most churches use a composite of the two. But many Christians add a doxology, a line of praise that was probably not in the original prayer: "For the kingdom, the power, and the glory are yours, now and forever."[1]

Ironically, Protestants, who tend to disparage tradition and stress "Scripture alone" are the ones who consistently add this doxology to the prayer. But Roman Catholics, who accept more readily the authority of later tradition, do not usually include it, except in inter-denominational settings (out of deference to Protestants) and, most importantly, in the Mass. There, however, following the eucharistic prayer, the Our Father is prayed by the congregation and ends with "deliver us from evil." The priest alone continues: "Deliver us, Lord, from every evil, and grant us peace in our day. In your mercy keep us free from sin and protect us from all anxiety as we wait in joyful hope for the coming of our Savior, Jesus Christ"—which nicely captures the expectation of the kingdom that characterizes the Lord's Prayer. Then the priest and people together pray, "For the kingdom, the power and the glory are yours, now and forever." In this way the doxology is used, but separated, to distinguish it from the actual prayer of Jesus.

Why were these words added to the Lord's Prayer?

By Jewish custom prayers ended with an expression of praise and adoration to God. Many scholars think that a doxology was added from the very beginning, though the wording presumably varied.

The best reason for including this doxology in the Lord's Prayer is that it fits. The prayer of Jesus, though simple, touches the nerve of faith and life so deeply that we instinctively feel the urge to praise God. The Father's great love for us, and our love and respect for the Father, prompt it. I have already noted how praise and thanksgiving are powerful undercurrents throughout Jesus's prayer, starting with the words "Our Father." What has been implied but left unspoken is now given voice, as though we cannot restrain ourselves any longer. So we unleash our praise to God.

In his introduction to the Psalms, Claus Westermann writes, "Forgetting God and turning away from God always begins when praise has been silenced. The secret of praise is the power it has to make connection with God; through praise one remains with God."[2]

Most churches in the West are not known for their excessive praise. In this respect we may have much to learn from some

of the younger churches in developing countries and from some
U.S. churches that are historically black or Pentecostal.

Christianity is growing faster in Africa today than in any other
region of the world, and indigenous Pentecostal churches are the
fastest growing element
of African Christian-
ity. Most members of
these churches are very
poor, and many people
attracted to them are
sick and need healing.
But worship in these
indigenous African
churches is character-
ized by hours of exuberant singing and sometimes dancing. The
hymns are mostly songs of praise. People come to church with
heavy burdens and hopes for healing, but they sing and sing and
sing God's praises. Many find healing, spiritual power and emotional release in praising God's goodness and mercy. In a world
that is harsh and oppressive for them, their uninhibited joy in
the Savior reflects a longing for the kingdom that may capture
much better than most of us do the hope that drives this prayer
of Jesus.

> *Father, we are surrounded by the majesty of your creation and the miracle of life. You care for us. You have redeemed us and given us the kingdom. Praise be to you now and forever!*

The hope that drives the prayer and each of its petitions is
one that looks forward to the final revelation of God's kingdom,
power, and glory, when the entire plan of salvation will be brought
to completion for all to see. This doxology acts as an exclamation
mark for that hope.

The doxology anchors that hope in God, for God alone can
make it come to pass. The kingdom, the power, and the glory all
belong to God. None of it belongs to us. So we put everything we
have prayed for into the Father's hands—again—not because the
Father needs to be reminded of this, but because *we* need to be

reminded, and in being reminded, entrust all of it to God. Nothing gives the Father more joy.

The kingdom, the power, and the glory of God are eternal, and we have been invited into God's presence to enjoy them fully. Why should we give our lives to any lesser purpose? Whatever else we pursue, we lose. But if God and God's kingdom are the great reality, then our every ambition, love, and loyalty must be understood in the light of it and be subordinate to it. How changed these aspirations become when they are given to God. They are filled with eternity. Our earthly responsibilities are ennobled and transformed by a vision in which compassion, justice, and generosity—that is to say, the purposes of God—replace our own purposes.

One way to avoid longing for our own kingdom, power, and glory is to concentrate on enhancing the well-being and reputation of others. And in so doing we honor the one who truly has the kingdom, the power, and the glory.

"For the kingdom, the power, and the glory are yours, now and forever" is a "Yes" to each of the petitions.

It is a "Yes" to the Father, our *Abba*, who loves us so.

It is a "Yes" to the honoring of God's holy name in all that we think and do.

It is a "Yes" to the kingdom and our desire to seek it first, and therefore a "Yes" to putting our will into the better hands of God.

It is a "Yes" to the Father for supplying us with every bodily need and the trust in him that sets us free to help others in their need.

It is a "Yes" to God's forgiveness and our willingness to forgive others.

It is a "Yes" to God's help in the face of every temptation, every evil, every challenge.

And it is praise to God alone for all of this.

Amen! Yes, it is so. And it shall be so.

13. A Few Suggestions

Sometimes the use of simple variations in the way we pray the prayer of Jesus can help us avoid getting stuck in a rut. There are many ways of doing this, and each person can discover a few that work well for him or her. Here are several that may be helpful or may stimulate thought of something better.

In my own private use of the prayer I have found that simply varying the position of the prayer helps. More often than not I use it at the end of my prayers, gathering mentally the persons and concerns that I have lifted up to God as I pray and reflect on each petition. But sometimes I begin with the Lord's Prayer and anticipate the people and needs that I will be praying for by name. At other times I use each petition of the prayer to pray more extensively for specific people in distress, family members, or those doing special service in the church or the world, and so forth. Sometimes I use the petitions of the prayer of Jesus to shape all of my prayers for the day.

N. T. Wright suggests dividing the prayer into seven parts and using one part or petition as the focus for each day of the week. Sunday: "Our Father." Monday: "May your holy name be honored," etc. "Use the clause of the day as your private retreat, into which you can step at any moment, through which you can pray for the people you meet, the things you're doing, all that's going on around you. The 'prayer of the day' then becomes the lens through which you see the world."[1]

At least for me, using the prayer of Jesus in different ways brings new understanding to my praying and my life.

Change of body language—kneeling, standing, moving about, riding a bus or train, lifting up hands, or praying aloud, for example—can also help. I do part of my praying while walking or jogging early in the morning, and I find that praying aloud in privacy at home often heightens my senses. What may seem awkward to one may be just right for another.

One of the readers of the initial draft of this book told me he found that some of his most edifying prayers came when he typed his thoughts on a word processor. "It helps me put my concerns in perspective and reorder my plans in response to God," he said. I've not prayed that way, but sometimes when praying (often aloud) I stumble across a new way of understanding or expressing something. I may scribble it down so I don't forget it. Some pieces of this book started that way.

Of course, these things take time. Almost anything useful does.

Variation can be applied in our corporate use of the Lord's Prayer as well. In some ancient rites, now revived, the priest prays one line of the prayer, and the congregation repeats it. This has the advantage of giving everyone a little time to think more deeply about what each petition means. Or a pastor can simply instruct the congregation to pray it very slowly and pause briefly between petitions. It will stand out. Having people open their hands, palms up, during the prayer (with or without raised arms) is also a way of setting it apart.

Another of my readers keeps in mind those with whom he is praying, so the petitions relate not to everyone in general (and no one in particular) but to those who are actually praying the prayer together at any given time. It can be a congregation or a meeting or a family. And it can call to mind specific persons. He says "the very attempt to do this heightens my attention to what I am praying. It may result in one petition standing out as particularly meaningful with respect to those with whom I'm now praying." This idea never occurred to me, but I find that it helps.

Another reader stressed the value of reflecting on each petition or on individual words. In this way, the private praying of the prayer can also link it to corporate prayer. He cited, for example, the word *Our* [Father]: "How do I pray this prayer with others in my church? in my family? in my denomination? How did I pray it with others now departed? How often do I pray it thinking only of myself and not of the 'us' that runs through the whole prayer and the 'our' that sets the prayer in that direction right from the beginning?"

You may have found a different way of becoming more engaged in the use of this prayer, or a way in which the prayer has helped you. If so, write and tell me about it. You can use the mailing address of Bread for the World found on the royalty page in the front of the book.

Chapter Notes

Chapter 1: A Confession

1. I have bracketed this because it was added later and does not appear in the earliest manuscripts. See chapter 12.

Chapter 2: "Lord, Teach Us to Pray"

1. Walter Wangerin, Jr., "Mother, you who pray, be radiant!" *The Lutheran*, May 1996, 6.
2. Cited by Millard Fuller, *Building Materials for Life* (Macon, Georgia: Smyth & Helwys, 2002), 31.
3. Henri J. M. Nouwen, *With Open Hands* (New York: Ballentine, 1985), 39.

Chapter 3: Our Father in Heaven

1. I have used this illustration in *How Much Is Enough? Hungering for God in an Affluent Culture* (Grand Rapids, Mich.: Baker Book House, 2003), 174.
2. See N. T. Wright, *The Lord & His Prayer* (Grand Rapids, Mich.: Eerdmans, 1996), 14-17.
3. William Sloane Coffin, *Credo* (Louisville: Westminster John Knox Press, 2004), 11.

Chapter 4: May Your Holy Name Be Honored

1. The verbs in these first three petitions are rare third person passive imperatives, all in the aorist tense, indicating a one-time event that is lasting. For this reason many scholars make the case that the petitions (along with the other three petitions, second person imperatives in the aorist tense) are anticipating the last day, when all will be fulfilled. They are exclamations. So this petition would be saying something like, "The day come when your holy name is completely honored by all!" This understanding underscores the grounding of the prayer (and Jesus's mission) on our ultimate hope in the kingdom fully revealed.

2. Brother Lawrence of the Resurrection, *The Practice of the Presence of God*, translated by John J. Delaney (New York: Doubleday, 1977), 49.

3. My own translation.

4. Clarence Jordan, *The Substance of Faith* (Association Press, 1972), 135. Cited by James Mulholland, *Praying Like Jesus: The Lord's Prayer in a Culture of Prosperity* (San Francisco: HarperSanFrancisco, 2001), 37.

5. Reported to me by a third party and confirmed by Tony Campolo in a letter to me dated August 30, 2004.

6. Millard Fuller, *Building Materials for Life* (Macon, Georgia: Smyth & Helwys, 2002), 35.

7. Stephen Carter in "Roundtable on Religion in Politics," *Tikkun*, Vol. 15, No. 6, 26.

8. Dianne Coluccio, "Extending Our Hands, Serving God's People—A Matter of Choices!" *Good News: The Pro Sanctity Movement Newsletter,* Winter-Spring 2003. Web address: www.prosancity.org.

9. Jimmy Allen, "The Tears of God," *Christian Ethics Today*, February 2002, 6-7.

10. Michael Leahy, "His Moment of Truth," *The Washington Post Magazine,* June 29, 2003, 10.

11. Gary Wills, *Why I Am a Catholic* (New York: Houghton Mifflin, 2002), 334.

Chapter 5: Your Kingdom Come

1. Certain according to God's plan, but I think we underestimate the humanity of Jesus if we think the outcome was all mapped out in his mind. Then his temptation, his struggle, his placing himself fully in our shoes, and his amazing trust in the Father seem less than real and complete.

2. Helen C. Crane, "Sacred Moments," *Maryknoll* magazine, April, 1999, 40.

3. Richard J. Foster, *Celebration of Discipline* (New York: Harper & Row, 1978), 35.

4. Martin Luther, *The Large Catechism*, in *The Book of Concord*, edited by Theodore G. Tappert (Philadelphia: Muhlenberg Press, 1959), 424.

5. George Appleton, Gen. ed., *The Oxford Book of Prayer* (Oxford University Press, 1986), 114.

6. Thomas Merton, *Thoughts in Solitude* (New York: Dell, 1958), 67 and 35.

7. C. S. Lewis, *Mere Christianity* (New York: Macmillan, 1953), 104.

8. Richard Rohr, quoted by John M. Fife in an untitled sermon at Southside Presbyterian Church, Tucson, Arizona, Sept. 16, 2001.

9. Dietrich Bonhoeffer, *Ethics,* edited by Eberhard Bethge, translated by Neville Horton Smith (London: SCM Press, 1955), 63.

Chapter 6: Your Will Be Done

1. William Sloane Coffin, *Credo* (Louisville: Westminster John Knox Press, 2004), 132.

2. Paul Scherer, *Love Is a Spendthrift* (New York: Harper & Brothers, 1961), 171.

3. From conversation with Robin Sonnenberg and an article by Roger R. Sonnenberg, "Unequally Yoked," *The Lutheran Witness*, September 1995, 5.

4. Desmond Mpilo Tutu, *No Future Without Forgiveness* (New York: Doubleday, 1997), cited by Jon Marc Taylor, letter to me dated April 18, 2004.

5. Jo Anne Lyon, *The Ultimate Blessing: Rediscovering the Power of God's Presence* (Indianapolis: Wesleyan, 2003), 85-86.

Chapter 7: Give Us Daily Bread—I

1. For example, Joachim Jeremias, *The Lord's Prayer*, translated by John Reumann (Philadelphia: Fortress Press, 1964), 23-26. Others say the petition reflects Israel's experience of receiving *manna* each morning, but only enough for each day; and that "tomorrow" may reflect the fact that workers got paid at sundown so they would have money for the next day's food.

2. Leslie F. Brandt, *Jesus/Now* (St. Louis: Concordia, 1978), 107.

3. Leslie F. Brandt, *Psalms/Now* (St. Louis: Concordia, 1973), 179.

4. James Mulholland, *Praying Like Jesus* (San Francisco: HarperCollins, 2001), 73.

5. I have written more extensively on this in *How Much Is Enough? Hungering for God in an Affluent Culture* (Grand Rapids, Mich.: Baker, 2003).

6. Marva J. Dawn, *Unfettered Hope: A Call to Faithful Living in an Affluent Society* (Louisville: Westminster John Knox, 2003), 177.

7. Dietrich Bonhoeffer, *The Cost of Discipleship*, translated by R.H. Fuller (New York: Macmillan, 1963), 148.

8. David Becker, 1931–2004.

9. Quoted in *The Living Pulpit*, October-December 2002, 35.

10. Joni Eareckson Tada, *The God I love: A Lifetime of Walking with Jesus* (Grand Rapids, Mich.: Zondervan, 2003), cited in a review by Cindy Crosby in *Christianity Today*, August 2003, 50.

11. Dietrich Bonhoeffer, from the hymn, "By Gracious Powers," translated by Fred Pratt Green, *With One Voice* (Minneapolis: Augsburg Fortress, 1995), hymn 736.

12. *Lutheran Book of Worship* (Minneapolis: Augsburg, 1978), hymn 229.

Chapter 8: Give Us Daily Bread—II

1. I have used this illustration in *How Much Is Enough? Hungering for God in an Affluent Culture* (Grand Rapids, Mich.: Baker Book House, 2003), 75.

2. Mary Murphy, letter to the author, January 19, 2004.

3. James Mulholland, *Praying Like Jesus* (San Francisco: Harper-Collins, 2001), 82.

4. Daniel Kadlec, "Quiet Giver," *Time,* September 17, 2001, 62-63.

5. Unpublished interview by Don McClanen and Bryan Sirchio of Harvest Time, April 11, 2003.

6. James Fallows, "The Invisible Poor," *The New York Times Magazine,* March 19, 2000, 68.

7. Dom Helder Camara, *Revoluton through Peace* (New York: Harper & Row, 1971), cited by Gladys M. Hunt, "Evangelism and Simpler Life Style," in *Living More Simply,* ed. Ronald J. Sider (Downers Grove, Ill.: InterVarsity, 1980), 171.

8. Craig L. Nessan, *Give Us This Day: A Lutheran Proposal for Ending World Hunger* (Minneapolis: Augsburg Fortress, 2003).

Chapter 9: Forgive As We Forgive—I

1. Edward Waldo Emerson, *Henry Thoreau, As Remembered by a Young Friend* (Houghton, 1917), 117f. Quoted by Bernard W. Anderson, *Rediscovering the Bible* (Haddam House, 1951), 180. I am indebted to Edward Simons for calling this to my attention.

2. Although this account is not in the oldest manuscripts, it has the ring of truth.

3. Cited by Thomas Cahill, *Pope John XXIII* (New York: Viking Penguin, 2002), 212.

4. Lewis B. Smedes, *The Art of Forgiving* (New York: Ballentine, 1996), 167-78.

5. J. R. Veneroso, M. M., "O Gentle God of Vengeance," and "Seeing I-to-I Again," *Maryknoll* magazine, Sept., 1999, 20-21.

6. Timothy C. Morgan, "Healing Genocide," *Christianity Today,* April 2004, 83.

7. C. S. Lewis, *Mere Christianity* (New York: Macmillan, 1953), 90-91.

Chapter 10: Forgive As We Forgive—II

1. Lewis B. Smedes, *Forgive & Forget* (New York: Pocket Books, 1984), 189.

2. Philip Yancey, *What's So Amazing about Grace?* (Grand Rapids, Mich.: Zondervan, 1997), 14. Italics mine.

3. Alicia C. Shepard, "A Mother's Courage," an op ed article in *The Washington Post,* January 11, 2003.

4. For a more detailed account, see Rachel King, *Don't Kill in Our Names* (New Brunswick: Rutgers University Press, 2003), 189-223.

Chapter 11: Deliver Us from Evil

1. See Philip B. Harner, *Understanding the Lord's Prayer* (Philadelphia: Fortress Press, 1975), 106-113.

2. I have replaced "good and evil" with "everything" because the expression, "knowing good and evil," in other places in the Old Testament means knowing everything from A to Z (omniscience).

3. See Rom. 5:12-21, and 1 Corinthians 15:45-49.

4. I made the same point in almost identical words in *How Much Is Enough? Hungering for God in an Affluent Culture* (Grand Rapids, Mich.: Baker Book House, 2003), 90.

5. David Cho, "Redskins' Gibbs Keeps the Faith," *The Washington Post,* April 11, 2004, page 1-A.

6. Roland H. Bainton, *Here I Stand* (New York: Abingdon-Cokesbury, 1950), 364-65.

7. Deborah Smith Douglas, *The Praying Life: Seeking God in All Things* (Harrisburg: Morehouse Publishing, 2003), x.

8. Charles Swindoll, *God's Provision in Time of Need,* quoted in "Reflections," *Christianity Today,* January 12, 1998, page 49.

9. Rick Warren, *The Purpose Driven Life* (Grand Rapids, Mich.: Zondervan, 2002), 201.

10. "The Appeal of 'Normal' Holiness," *The Word among Us,* September 2004, 5-8.

Chapter 12: The Kingdom, Power, and Glory Are Yours

1. It is included in the King James Version, but not in recent translations that go by the oldest manuscripts.

2. Claus Westermann, *The Psalms: Structure, Content and Message* (Minneapolis: Augsburg, 1980), 6.

Chapter 13: A Few Suggestions

1. N. T. Wright, *The Lord & His Prayer* (Grand Rapids, Mich.: Eerdmans, 1996), 8-9.

Other Resources from Augsburg

The Perfect Prayer by Philip Mathias
224 pages, 0-8066-5156-3

The basis for *The Perfect Prayer* is the shorter version of
Jesus's prayer found in Luke's Gospel. Philip Mathias
examines each of the six petitions of the Lord's Prayer to
explore the role it plays in the prayer's aspiration: the coming
of the kingdom of God, which is the core of Christian joy.

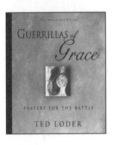

Guerrillas of Grace by Ted Loder
136 pages, 0-8066-9054-2

For nearly two decades, this classic collection of tough,
beautiful, and earthy prayers has lightened hearts and dared
spirits to soar.

Soul Weavings by Lyn Klug
160 pages, 0-8066-2849-9

A collection of rich, strong prayers that reflect the needs and
experiences of women of all ages. They are gathered from
historic and contemporary women of faith from around the
world.

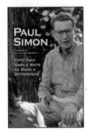

Fifty-Two Simple Ways to Make a Difference by Paul Simon
144 pages, 0-8066-4678-0

A practical and inspiring book for general readers that reminds
us that the little things we do count, and offers concrete
suggestions for small ways of making a difference.

Available wherever books are sold.